Safeguarding and Child Protection for Nurses, Midwives and Health Visitors

A practical guide

Safeguarding and Child Protection for Nurses, Midwives and Health Visitors

A practical guide

Catherine Powell

Mc Graw Hill   Open University Press

Open University Press
McGraw-Hill Education
McGraw-Hill House
Shoppenhangers Road
Maidenhead
Berkshire
England
SL6 2QL

email: enquiries@openup.co.uk
world wide web: www.openup.co.uk

and Two Penn Plaza, New York, NY 10121-2289, USA

First published 2011

A catalogue record of this book is available from the British Library

ISBN-13: 978-0-33-523614-5 (pb) 978-0-33-523613-8 (hb)
ISBN-10: 0335236146 (pb) 0335236138 (hb)
e-ISBN: 9780335240302

Library of Congress Cataloging-in-Publication Data
CIP data applied for

Typeset by Aptara Inc., India

Fictitous names of companies, products, people, characters and/or data that may be used herein (in case studies or in examples) are not intended to represent any real individual, company, product or event.

Printed and bound by CPI Group (UK) Ltd, Croydon, CR0 4YY

The *McGraw·Hill* Companies

For my father, Harry Schorah, who made children happy.
1928–2011

Contents

Abbreviations

ADD	attention deficit disorder
CAF	Common Assessment Framework
CAMHS	child and adolescent mental health services
CBT	cognitive behavioural therapy
CDOP	child death overview panel
CEOP	Child Exploitation and Online Protection Centre
CMACE	Centre for Maternal and Child Enquiries
DOSC	designated officer for safeguarding children
FII	fabricated or induced illness
FNP	Family Nurse Partnership
FSID	Foundation for the Study of Infant Deaths
ICPC	initial child protection conference
ICT	information and communication technology
IRO	independent reviewing officer
LSCB	Local Safeguarding Children Board
MAPPA	multi-agency public protection arrangements
MARAC	multi-agency risk assessment conferencing
NAHI	non-accidental head injury
NICE	National Institute for Health and Clinical Excellence
NMC	Nursing and Midwifery Council
NPSA	National Patient Safety Agency
NSPCC	National Society for the Prevention of Cruelty to Children
ODD	oppositional defiant disorder
Ofsted	Office for Standards in Education
PCT	Primary Care Trust
PICU	paediatric intensive care unit
RCM	Royal College of Midwives
RCN	Royal College of Nursing
RCPC	review child protection conference
RCPCH	Royal College of Paediatrics and Child Health
SIDS	sudden infant death syndrome
SIRI	serious incident requiring investigation
SUDI	sudden unexpected death in infancy
TAC	team around the child

Introduction

Safeguarding and child protection is a vital role for the nursing, midwifery and health visiting professions; we are a large and potent workforce with a range of opportunities to make a difference. Our strength is that we bridge universal and specialist services in maternity, child health, mental health, learning disabilities and adult health. Our practice takes place with children, young people and their families. We understand that there are a broad range of behaviours in the way in which families function. Because of this we are in an excellent position to spot situations that may fall outside of the norm and threaten the safety and well-being of children.

However, if you are a nursing, midwifery or specialist community public health student[1] or a newly-qualified practitioner, the chances are that you may be feeling anxious about 'getting it right'. You may also be overwhelmed by the vast array of local and national policies and procedures that provide the statutory framework in which you are expected to practise. The over-arching purpose of this practical text is thus to develop your safeguarding and child protection knowledge, skills and competence so that you can help to ensure that the potential of the professions' contribution to ensuring the safety and well-being of children and young people is realized.

The book is primarily aimed at nursing and midwifery students and newly-qualified professionals, who will ultimately be accountable for their safeguarding and child protection practice. However, it is likely that there will be more experienced practitioners, perhaps those working essentially with adult groups, who have had little opportunity to develop their knowledge, skills and competence in safeguarding children. These practitioners may find that this book offers new perspectives on their role and the expectations placed upon them to recognize and respond to concerns about a child. Another important group will be those 'returning to practice', especially those who are returning to health visiting practice as part of the current drive to recruit more health visitors. These 'returners' may find that their safeguarding and child protection knowledge is a little rusty. In addition, there will be those from outside the nursing and midwifery professions who would like to understand the potential safeguarding contribution of these professionals. In short, this practical text may appeal to a wider professional audience than is initially evident.

Promoting the welfare of children and young people, and ensuring that they are protected from harm is, in my view, one of the most challenging,

---

[1]The specialist community public health nurse part of the Nursing and Midwifery Council (NMC) Register includes health visitors and school nurses.

yet also rewarding, aspects of professional practice. Work in safeguarding children cuts across 'branches', 'sub-disciplines', 'specialities' and 'settings'. It places nurses, midwives and health visitors as valued partners within the context of multi-professional and inter-agency working; especially in partnership with colleagues from children's social care, the police and education. Safeguarding children is a key public health function and it is a whole-profession responsibility.

It is fair to say that good safeguarding children practice across all agencies remains largely hidden and unannounced; after all, it is difficult to capture evidence of successfully *preventing* harm. However, anyone whose work brings them into contact with families may come across situations that present a significant risk to children and young people and (rarely) the serious injury or death of a child from abuse or neglect. Reviews of such cases may offer insights into good practice, as well as opportunities for improvements.

This book recognizes that safeguarding and child protection is a public health issue that encompasses a wide range of professional activities, including:

- preventative work;
- holistic assessment;
- early identification of need;
- provision of parenting support;
- recognition and referral of children who are at risk of, or are suffering from, significant harm;
- working with a multi-agency team to provide additional support and monitoring as part of a 'child in need' plan or a 'child protection plan'; and
- child death and serious case review.

Importantly, a key message for the nursing and midwifery professions is that the skills needed to achieve good safeguarding practice are very similar to the skills needed to be a good nurse or midwife. As I argued in my previous book, nursing and midwifery share some of the core attributes of successful safeguarding practice: 'assessing need, working in partnership with individual children and young people, their families and multi-disciplinary teams to promote physical and emotional well-being and ensure safety' (Powell 2007: 15–16).

Practice is at the heart of this book. In my own practice I see daily examples of the challenging and emotionally demanding work that nurses, midwives and health visitors undertake at the front line to ensure that children and young people are safe and healthy. Their achievements are often remarkable, but there is always more to do. In the words of the late Tony Morrison (2009), my aim as a consultant nurse has always been to act as a 'scholar-facilitator' – promoting excellence in evidence-informed practice. In doing so, I find that the best learning comes from reflecting on the reality of practice and the *stories* of the families and professionals involved. This book is thus based on case scenarios in practice. These are, for obvious reasons, fictitious cases, but the events described are all based on reality; the experiences of children, young people, families and professionals who I have been privileged to meet in practice and from whom we can learn so much.

The first chapter considers the *underpinning principles and frameworks* for safeguarding and child protection practice. This includes a brief overview of contemporary policy and the professional mandate for this work. While the book concerns the safeguarding and child protection work of nurses, midwives and health visitors, this chapter also introduces the roles of others, including the statutory lead agencies (children's social care and the police).

Chapter 2 considers the roles of nurses and midwives in *prevention and early intervention* and reflects the importance of ensuring the right support and help for children, young people and families with additional needs. The three case scenarios discuss a pregnant 16-year-old, who is referred to the family nurse partnership, a family struggling to cope with the demands of parenting two small boys and a young teenager who is under pressure from her boyfriend to have a sexual relationship. A midwife, a health visitor and a school nurse feature.

Chapter 3 considers *physical abuse* and the process of referral of a child protection concern to children's social care. The three case scenarios discuss a 10-week-old baby who presents with a bruise, a 14-month-old child with suspicious burns and a 6-year-old who is presenting with possible fabricated illness. A practice nurse, an emergency nurse practitioner and a paediatric nurse are key care providers.

Chapter 4 considers *emotional abuse* and the process of the initial child protection conference. The three case scenarios discuss a 6-year-old child described by her mother as 'difficult to love', a 13-year-old who is missing school because she is caring for her younger siblings and a 9-year-old child with cerebral palsy who is somewhat excluded from family life. These cases receive care from a child and adolescent mental health practitioner, a school nurse and a community children's nurse.

Chapter 5 considers *sexual abuse* and the professional contribution to a child protection plan. The three case scenarios discuss a 14-year-old attending a young person's sexual health clinic, a 10-year-old with a progressive neurological disorder and an adult mental health client who discloses accessing child pornography on the internet. Care is provided by a sexual health nurse, a learning disability nurse and an adult mental health nurse.

Chapter 6 considers *neglect* and the decision-making process at a child protection review conference. The three case scenarios discuss a newborn baby at risk of neglect because of his mother's lifestyle, 18-month-old twins who have been subject to a child protection plan because of concerns about their health and development and a 4-year-old who was admitted to a paediatric intensive care unit after accidentally ingesting an opiate substitute. Practitioners involved in the cases include a midwife, a health visitor and a substance misuse worker.

Chapter 7 considers *statutory child death review* and *serious case review* processes. The cases discussed reflect a sudden unexpected death and a non-accidental head injury in an infant. Nurses, midwives and health visitors may be asked to contribute to child death and serious case review processes, albeit that they will be led and supported by safeguarding children specialists. The chapter focuses on the nursing leadership roles in safeguarding and child protection.

The final chapter, Chapter 8, pulls together the *key learning* with some messages for the future.

Throughout the book there are 'Practice points', 'Practice questions' and 'Markers of good practice' to stimulate further thinking and application to real-life practice. Each chapter ends with a summary and a number of key points to support practitioner learning.

Whether you are a student, a newly-qualified practitioner, an experienced practitioner who is seeking to improve their safeguarding children knowledge and skills, you are returning to practice or you have an interest in the potential of the contribution of the nursing and midwifery professions, I hope that you will find this text helpful. Your contribution to keeping children and young people safe is vital; as is your ability to provide good support to parents and to parenting. You will have a range of opportunities to make a difference; you may even save a life.

Principles for practice

Learning outcomes

This chapter will help you to:

- Define key terms – i.e. child, childhood, parenting, safeguarding, child protection and child maltreatment.
- Understand why the needs of the child or young person take priority in decision-making in practice.
- Recognize the statutory and professional duty to safeguard and promote the welfare of children within a context of inter-agency working.
- Map safeguarding and child protection practice to a public health model that promotes prevention.
- Use the remaining chapters to support and inform your knowledge, skills and competence in safeguarding children practice.

Introduction

The aim of this book is to prepare and support nursing and midwifery practitioners to achieve excellence and to confirm the importance of safeguarding and child protection in their professional role. It is intended for nursing, midwifery and specialist community public health nursing students, qualified practitioners, those 'returning to practice' (especially health visitors) and those with an interest in the professional contribution of this workforce. Above all, it is about supporting best outcomes for children and young people; especially in ensuring their health, safety and well-being.

This opening chapter outlines the principles for safeguarding children practice and provides the foundation for an understanding of the content and context of this book. Key terms are defined, and the legislation and statutory frameworks for developing and supporting professional practice are introduced, as are the roles of other key players in the field. The aim of the chapter is to 'set the scene' for the case studies and practice scenarios that will show how nurses, midwives and health visitors can, and do, play a major role in safeguarding and child protection. This is achieved through a brief review of the underpinning knowledge for practice.

Children and young people

The UK has adopted the legal definition of a child as being an individual who has not yet reached the age of 18 years. This is in line with the United Nations Convention on the Rights of the Child 1989[1] (hereafter referred to as the UN Convention) and is the definition used within the UK's safeguarding guidance, policy and legislation. The definition applies to all children and young people, including those who are living independently, are in the armed forces, in secure custodial accommodation or in further education. Furthermore, statutory safeguarding children guidance specifically notes that the definition also applies to those in hospital (HM Government 2010). This is important because health care traditions in the UK mean that individuals aged 16 and 17 years are most likely to be cared for in 'adult settings'.[2] In these circumstances young people are likely to receive their care from those whose preparation for practice has been focused on 'adults' and who are perhaps less well briefed, or focused, on their safeguarding and child protection responsibilities.

It is also important to consider the other 'end' of the age spectrum – i.e. the unborn infant. While unborn infants (of any gestation) are not legally defined as children, their need for protection from harm must still be considered in cases where there is concern about expectant parents' ability to ensure the safety and well-being of their child. This would primarily be a responsibility of the midwife and other professionals providing care in the ante-natal period. Because such concerns can relate to substance misuse and/or adult mental health problems, practitioners working in these fields also need to be aware of their responsibilities to recognize and respond to the risks to the child. It is also pertinent to note that in some cases the 'parent to be' may be a child themselves.

Childhood is clearly a time of rapid, if sometimes uneven, maturity in a multi-faceted range of attributes, including those relating to physical, psychological, intellectual, emotional and social development. Nevertheless, despite the fact that the term 'child' legally applies up until the age of 18 years, this label may not be well-received by those developmentally maturing individuals approaching the end of their childhood! Clinical guidelines on child maltreatment commissioned by the National Institute for Health and Clinical Excellence (NICE) (often referred to as the 'NICE guidelines') offer the definitions outlined below (NCCWCH 2009: 1), and these will be broadly reflected within this book:

- Infant: aged under 1 year
- Child: aged under 13 years
- Young person: aged 13–17 years

---

[1] Children and young people's protective, welfare and participative rights are reflected in the United Nations Convention on the Rights of the Child, which was adopted by the General Assembly of the United Nations on 20 November 1989 and ratified by the UK in 1991.
[2] Child and adolescent mental health services (CAMHS) being a notable exception.

Practice question

What do you think are the particular care and development needs of individuals within each of the above age groups throughout their journey into adulthood?

Children's rights

Children and young people's rights to provision for welfare and protection from harm, detailed within the UN Convention, are a useful starting point for developing an understanding of what needs to happen in practice to ensure that actions are taken to safeguard and promote their welfare. The UN Convention outlines the responsibilities of governments to provide the best possible services to support children to achieve their full potential into adulthood (i.e. through health, education and social care provision) and address inequalities between children and adults (e.g. right to physical integrity).

The UN Convention has four core principles:

- Non-discrimination
- Devotion to the best interests of the child
- The right to life, survival and development
- Respect for the views of the child

Crucially, the document provides a mandate for the development of a rights-based approach to safeguarding and child protection policy, legislation and guidance, and this is reflected in the UK. International readers will need to find out how their governments have enshrined the principles of the UN Convention within their own country's safeguarding and child protection framework.[3]

Importantly, the UN Convention seeks to ensure that children are seen *and* heard. In his report into progress made in safeguarding and child protection post the Victoria Climbié tragedy, Laming (2009) argues that the child's perspective, experience and well-being are central to any assessment of need within a family. The key message for practice is that children's rights, child-centredness and the voice of the child are essential to the delivery of safe, effective care and the achievement of best outcomes. This will be a theme throughout the book.

Parents and parenting

Safeguarding children is often promoted as being 'everyone's responsibility' but it is important to note that it is primarily the role and responsibility of parents (or others who hold parental responsibility for, or have care of, a child). In recognition of this, recent statutory guidance states that while there is 'no single, perfect way to bring up children' (HM Government 2010: 29)

---

[3] At the time of writing the UN Convention has been ratified in all countries in the world apart from Somalia and the USA.

there are fundamental aspects of good parenting that can be seen to support the rights of children. These include:

> Caring for children's basic needs, keeping them safe and protected, being attentive and showing them warmth and love, encouraging them to express their views and consistently taking these into account, and providing the stimulation needed for their development and to help them achieve their potential, within a stable environment where they experience consistent guidance and boundaries.
>
> (HM Government 2010: 29–30)

This description of what good parenting looks like is helpful for health professionals, and others, in determining what support may be needed for families by providing a benchmark for assessment of strengths and deficits, including potential risk of harm to children and young people. However, in most cases it will be the parents who will be encouraged to seek support and this recognition is important in determining which services (over and above universal provision) can be provided.

Practice question

What is the difference between supporting *parents* and supporting *parenting*?

Positive parenting

Adopting and promoting a 'positive parenting' approach, where good behaviour is rewarded, and bad behaviour ignored, is a strategy that can do much to improve the outcomes for children and contribute to happy and fulfilling parenting. This includes helping to prevent child maltreatment. Nurses, midwives and health visitors can help to support positive parenting and signpost parents to a range of programmes that can help to address this challenging role. An example of one such programme is given below.

Triple P programme: positive parenting and prevention of child maltreatment

The Triple P programme ('positive parenting programme': see www8. triplep.net) is an evidence-based initiative that is demonstrating a preventative effect with families who are at high risk of maltreating their children. Key facets of this programme include the development of children's emotional regulation and supporting and helping parents to become resourceful, independent problem-solvers. This is achieved through the use of individual and group sessions, and in the provision of materials to support learning and promote positive parenting techniques. Developed by an Australian psychologist, the programme is becoming well established across the UK.

Fatherhood

The roles and responsibilities of fathers in ensuring the health, safety and well-being of their children deserve a special mention. In the UK, the Fatherhood Institute takes a research-based approach to influencing policy and practice, including practice within health care. The Institute promotes the need for improvements in paternity provision and the inclusion of fathers in the delivery of services for children and young people. This has important implications for maternity services and broader child health provision, where arguably there has tended to be a woman/mother-centred approach to care provision and delivery.

The Fatherhood Institute website (www.fatherhoodinstitute.org) provides details of how unmarried fathers who do not automatically have legal rights and responsibilities for their child (i.e. parental responsibility) may obtain this. There is also an explanation of why this is important in the provision of parental consent for medical procedures and in gaining access to a child's health care records. It is notable that amendments to the original legislation concerning the position of fathers and parental responsibility (as per the Children Act 1989) have sought to promote greater inclusivity, and hopefully this will translate into the practice of all those working with children, young people and their families and impact favourably on family life.

Safeguarding and child protection

The terms 'safeguarding' and 'child protection' are not directly interchangeable because the notion of safeguarding both encompasses child protection, and embraces wider activity to support the well-being of children. This can be illustrated through the provision of preventative and early intervention strategies, such as positive parenting programmes and support. The following definition of safeguarding (HM Government 2010: 34), which links safeguarding with promoting the welfare of children, is taken from the statutory guidance for England:[4]

- protecting children from maltreatment;
- preventing impairment of children's health or development;
- ensuring that children are growing up in circumstances consistent with the provision of safe and effective care; and undertaking that role so as to enable those children to have optimum life chances and to enter adulthood successfully.

This definition reflects the move to an outcomes-based approach to children's policy and legislation and this is a strategy that has been broadly adopted in all the countries of the UK. The positive stance of the policy can be reflected through actions taken by nursing and midwifery professionals. These include

---

[4]In recognition that England has the largest population of children and young people, when compared with the other countries of the UK, this book will, for the most part, reflect English statutory guidance. The Appendix provides more details and signposts comparative documents for Wales, Scotland and Northern Ireland, albeit that there are many similarities across the UK as a whole.

the provision of help and advice to parents, as well as the promotion of healthy choices and well-being for their children.

Well-being is centred on achievement of the *Every Child Matters* policy outcomes (HM Government 2004), which are said to reflect 'what children and young people said they wanted' from their childhoods, i.e. to:

- be healthy;
- stay safe;
- enjoy and achieve;
- make a positive contribution;
- achieve economic well-being.

Although there is discrete guidance for the 'stay safe' outcome (HM Government 2008a), it is important to recognize that the five outcomes are linked and co-dependent – for example, a child who is not healthy may not enjoy and achieve and be able to enter adulthood successfully; a child who is harmed is likely to suffer consequences to their physical and/or emotional health and well-being and so on. The Children Act 2004 takes attainment of the five outcomes as core to its definition of 'well-being'.

Practice question

In line with statutory guidance, Local Safeguarding Children Boards (or their equivalent) produce local policies and procedures for inter-agency working to safeguard children. In addition, each health care organization will also have its own 'in house' policy and procedures. Are you aware of how to locate and use these documents in your locality?

Risks to children's well-being

The increased risks to children and young people's health, safety and well-being associated with parental mental health difficulties, substance misuse and/or domestic violence are widely acknowledged within contemporary policy. There is also striking evidence of these risks being greater for children of parents who have never worked, or are long-term unemployed, when compared to the children of those from professional or managerial classes. These factors have important ramifications for the commissioning and provision of equitable and accessible health services that seek to address inequalities in health.

Practice question

What is the role of your organization in addressing health inequalities in your locality?

Child maltreatment

Child maltreatment (also widely referred to as 'child abuse' and 'neglect') is a challenging concept to define, not least because what is, or is not, considered to be harmful to children can vary both over time and between individuals, according to their knowledge, beliefs and values (Corby 2006). The concept of child maltreatment refers both to the infliction of harm and failing to take action to prevent harm (HM Government 2010). In the UK child maltreatment is frequently categorized as 'physical, emotional or sexual abuse or neglect' although in reality these forms of maltreatment overlap and may co-exist.

Importantly, child maltreatment most commonly occurs within family settings with parents, or those in a parental role, the usual perpetrators. This fact is reflected in the case studies described in this book. However, child maltreatment can also occur in institutions (including hospitals) and within communities. Stranger abuse, although of strong interest in the media, and a source of much anxiety to parents, is relatively rare.

Practice point

It can be helpful to consider child maltreatment as part of a spectrum of 'poor to good parenting'. Nurses and midwives, who provide care to all families, are in a position where they can make judgements that benchmark the care of children with the non-maltreating majority. However, many prefer a definition that has a more clear-cut dividing line between behaviour that is indicative of abuse, and behaviour which is not. Either way, this is challenging territory and practitioners may face considerable debate with other professional or lay viewpoints when considering a possibility of maltreatment occurring within a family.

Significant harm

The context of harm and the longer-term effects on the victim are important factors in the assessment of child maltreatment, especially where decisions are to be made in relation to the threshold for statutory intervention in family life – i.e. the need to invoke child protection proceedings. The concept of 'significant harm', a term introduced by the Children Act 1989 (England and Wales), is important because it recognizes the need to consider a range of factors, including:

- the nature of harm;
- the impact on the health and development of the child;
- any special needs in the child (including disability or medical condition);
- the parental capacity to meet the needs of the child; and
- the context of the family and environment.

While stating that there are no absolute criteria to judge significant harm, the statutory guidance suggests that:

> Sometimes a single traumatic event may constitute significant harm, for example, a violent assault, suffocation or poisoning. More often, significant harm is a compilation of significant events, both acute and longstanding, which interrupt, change or damage the child's physical and psychological development. Some children live in circumstances where their health and development are neglected. For them, it is the corrosiveness of long-term emotional, physical or sexual abuse that causes impairment to the extent of constituting significant harm.
>
> (HM Government 2010: 8)

Reflecting on the 'daily lived experience' of the child can aid nurses' and midwives' professional judgement about whether or not a child is suffering significant harm. Clinical supervision is key.

The impact of child maltreatment

Recognizing and responding to concerns about possible child maltreatment is important in terms of the major impact that abuse and neglect have on health, both in, and beyond, childhood. This can include:

- death;
- neurological damage;
- disability;
- physical injuries;
- mental health problems (including depression and self-harm);
- poor self-esteem;
- attachment disorders;
- emotional and behavioural problems; and
- educational difficulties.

There is a need to acknowledge and promote awareness of the emerging findings of a body of research that links poor health and social outcomes in adulthood with child maltreatment. The 'adverse childhood events' studies (Felitti *et al.* 1998; Brown *et al.* 2009) provide a substantial evidence base to link maltreatment in childhood with the increased likelihood of smoking, alcoholism, substance misuse, depression, suicide attempts, sexual health problems, physical inactivity, severe obesity and risk of premature death in adulthood. While child protection professionals do acknowledge that there are some individuals who display a resilience to the effects of child abuse and neglect, the morbidity and mortality from what is essentially a preventable issue is clearly unacceptable.

The prevalence of child maltreatment

It is important for nurses, midwives and health visitors to understand the prevalence of child maltreatment, as well as its impact on the health of populations. The World Health Organization (WHO) (2006) estimates that child maltreatment is responsible for 0.6 per cent of all child deaths world-wide. Physical assault, especially non-accidental head injury, is the most common cause of such deaths, but neglect can also be an important factor. While child deaths from abuse by parents or carers are rare, and rates do appear to be declining in England and Wales (Pritchard and Williams 2009), such deaths are pivotal in informing the direction of policy and practice, especially where they have been in the public eye.

Perhaps less overtly debated are the studies that suggest that 1 in 10 of all children suffer from some form of maltreatment (physical, emotional, sexual abuse or neglect) during the course of their childhood (e.g. Cawson *et al.* 2000). The risk appears to be greatest in infancy, although research that has considered the learning from severe and fatal cases of child maltreatment has also identified that certain groups of young people (whose needs and distress have been described as being 'missed' or 'marginalized') can be extremely vulnerable too (Brandon *et al.* 2009).

Safeguarding children and public health

Successful safeguarding children work not only improves outcomes during childhood, but also the well-being of populations. The burden of ill health and poor outcomes from adverse events in childhood, including child maltreatment, is increasingly significant in countries such as the UK, where health and well-being are generally improving.

Safeguarding children and young people is thus a major public health issue that is increasingly recognized to require a public health solution. This point is taken up by Ferguson (2009) who notes that safeguarding is part of the continuum of care provided by a range of practitioners to families and that it sits comfortably within a health improvement model (at primary, secondary and tertiary levels of prevention). Such an approach, she suggests, builds capability and capacity and makes effective use of resources. It acknowledges that professionals, and indeed lay people, are well placed and well able to identify issues of concern about the safety and well-being of a child.

Ferguson argues that a public health approach is enabling and seeks to offer a range of practical support, training and supervision to front line staff with clear lines of accountability. Crucially it also allows a move from a 'disease model', where 'signs and symptoms' of child abuse were identified by health specialists and responsibility passed to statutory lead agencies, to one which engenders prevention and early intervention and empowers the family and a range of practitioners to work together towards positive outcomes for children. This approach is recognized throughout this book and is one that should sit comfortably with contemporary nursing and midwifery practice.

Skills and competencies for safeguarding and child protection practice

Thus far, this chapter has introduced some key definitions: child, childhood, parenting, safeguarding, child protection and child maltreatment.

Safeguarding children has been described within a public health framework which has in turn given nurses and midwives a mandate for prevention and early intervention, and proactive work with families, in addition to their responsibilities to recognize and respond to concerns that a child may be suffering from abuse or neglect.

The range of responsibilities is reflected in the professional input to the safeguarding and child protection processes, which include:

- the use of the Common Assessment Framework (CAF);
- making a referral to children's social care (social services);
- the strategy discussion;
- the initial child protection conference;
- the core group;
- the child protection review conference;
- the child death review processes;
- the serious case review processes.

Chapters 2 to 7 have been structured in a logical way that allows the above processes to be sequenced through the case studies. These will demonstrate that good communication and assessment skills, as well as knowledge of child care and development are important tools for good quality safeguarding and child protection work. However, to be really successful, nurses, midwives and health visitors need to develop the ability to practise in an authoritative manner. This has been described as being: 'urgent, thorough, challenging, with a low threshold of concern, keeping the focus on the child, and with high expectations of parenting and of what services should expect of themselves' (DfE 2010b: 68). Nursing and midwifery professionals and students are guided in practice by a professional code (NMC 2008, 2009a). This includes the mandate for their:

- professional duties in relation to protecting and promoting health and well-being in individuals, their families, carers and communities;
- advocacy for clients, including helping individuals to access to health and social care support and information; and
- the disclosure of information where it is believed that someone may be at risk of harm or posing a risk of harm (including a co-worker).

In addition to the above, the Nursing and Midwifery Council (NMC) *Code* (2008) is clear on the standards expected in relation to record-keeping. Record-keeping is a crucially important aspect of safeguarding children practice. As well as being clear, factual and contemporary accounts of the assessment and delivery of care, records should also demonstrate justification of decision-making, including that relating to sharing information with other practitioners and agencies. Nursing and midwifery records may be secured in cases of serious or fatal child abuse, and they can also be used in court proceedings. Poor record-keeping is a common theme in findings from serious case reviews. This includes the examples of: illegible signatures; failures of practitioners to give their designation (e.g. health visitor, community midwife, etc.); lack of clarity about assessment, decision-making, care planning and evaluation of care delivery; and, crucially, a *failure to reflect the views and wishes of the child*.

Practice question

How can you ensure that your record-keeping meets the required standard?

Recognizing and responding to child maltreatment

Despite the wealth of studies and literature that have sought to describe and measure child maltreatment, it is widely acknowledged that it remains under-recognized and under-reported. It is concerning that health professionals have been identified as being slow to recognize maltreatment and to respond appropriately, even where there are clear signs of abuse or neglect. The reasons for this (Gilbert *et al.* 2008) may include:

- poor knowledge;
- anxiety about relationships with families;
- uncertainty about the ability of statutory agencies (i.e. social care) to respond.

Through the case scenarios, this book seeks to promote a better understanding of the child protection process as well as the features of child maltreatment. Both are important if we are to meaningfully improve practice and impact on the needless morbidity and mortality that results from child maltreatment.

Although the case studies are built on the practice of nurses, midwives and health visitors, it is important to note that this practice takes place within an inter-agency context and together with professionals from a raft of statutory and voluntary organizations. The lead child protection agencies are children's social care and the police service and it is important to understand the roles and responsibilities of professionals from these agencies at the outset.

Local authority children's social care departments have a statutory duty to make enquiries if they have a reason to suspect that a child in their area is suffering, or at risk of suffering, significant harm. The child protection social worker is responsible for making enquiries and undertaking initial and core assessments. Social workers work closely with the police in undertaking enquiries, including joint interviewing of children and young people who may have suffered maltreatment. All children and young people who are 'subject to a child protection plan' will have an allocated social worker. As well as making a leading contribution to core groups and child protection conferences, the social worker may also work closely with their legal advisers in cases which go before the family courts.

Any police officer can support the need to take action to safeguard and promote the welfare of a child or young person through the use of the powers of police protection (see Chapter 3). However, all police forces also have a dedicated team of officers who have a statutory role in child protection and safeguarding. This will include investigating the criminal aspects of child abuse cases and working closely with colleagues from other agencies in sharing information and intelligence. Particular links are made with their work on domestic abuse and violence, including multi-agency risk assessment conferencing (MARAC) and multi-agency public protection arrangements (MAPPA). Police officers are involved in all unexpected deaths.

Information-sharing and inter-agency working

The notion of liaising with other agencies can raise concerns among health care practitioners about information-sharing practices. However, successful safeguarding often relies on 'piecing together' information from a variety of sources to get a clear picture of risks and strengths within a family. As noted above, most situations of significant harm to children and young people are related to a compilation of significant events.

In an effort to improve and support good practice in information-sharing a range of cross-government guides and training materials have been published to support the information-sharing principles outlined in *Working Together* (HM Government 2010).[5] These have been endorsed by leading professional organizations including the Royal College of Nursing (RCN), the Royal College of Midwives (RCM) and the Community Practitioners and the Health Visitors Association (CPHVA). In particular, the guides highlight 'seven golden rules' for information-sharing (HM Government 2008b: 11) shown below.

The seven golden rules for information-sharing

1 **Remember that the Data Protection Act is not a barrier to sharing information** but provides a framework to ensure that personal information about living persons is shared appropriately.

2 **Be open and honest** with the person (and/or their family where appropriate) from the outset about why, what, how and with whom information will, or could be shared, and seek their agreement, unless it is unsafe or inappropriate to do so.

---

[5] see: www.dcsf.gov.uk/everychildmatters/strategy/deliveringservices1/informationsharing.

3 **Seek advice** if you are in any doubt, without disclosing the identity of the person where possible.

4 **Share with consent where appropriate** and, where possible, respect the wishes of those who do not consent to share confidential information. You may still share information without consent if, in your judgement, that lack of consent can be overridden in the public interest. You will need to base your judgement on the facts of the case.

5 **Consider safety and well-being:** base your information-sharing decisions on considerations of the safety and well-being of the person and others who may be affected by their actions.

6 **Necessary, proportionate, relevant, accurate, timely and secure:** ensure that the information you share is necessary for the purpose for which you are sharing it, is shared only with those people who need to have it, is accurate and up-to-date, is shared in a timely fashion, and is shared securely.

7 **Keep a record** of your decision and the reasons for it – whether it is to share information or not. If you decide to share, then record what you have shared, with whom and for what purpose.

The roles of designated and named professionals

Advice and support for all aspects of safeguarding and child protection practice can be gained from nursing and midwifery safeguarding leads. These are known as 'designated' and 'named' professionals. According to statutory guidance: 'Each Primary Care Trust (PCT) is responsible for identifying a senior paediatrician and a senior nurse who will undertake the role of designated professionals for safeguarding children in commissioning services across the health economy' (HM Government 2010: 54). The key roles and responsibilities of these professionals include:

- provision of expert advice on safeguarding children to the PCT, local safeguarding children board, health professionals and other agencies;
- support and advice to named professionals;
- advice on the monitoring of the safeguarding children aspects of commissioning contracts;
- influencing and promoting single and inter-agency training;
- skilled involvement in safeguarding processes;
- reviewing and evaluating the practice and learning from serious case reviews (see Chapter 7).

All health care providers, whether NHS Trusts, Foundation Trusts, public, third or independent sector should also identify a named doctor and a named nurse (and named midwife where maternity services are provided). The focus for the named professionals is safeguarding within their own organization.

Named professionals have a key role in:

- promoting good practice and providing advice and expertise in safeguarding and child protection;
- supporting the clinical governance role of the organization by ensuring that audits on safeguarding are undertaken;
- ensuring that a training strategy is in place and is delivered within their own organization;
- conducting the organization's internal management reviews (see Chapter 7).

Practice question

Do you know the names and contact details for your named and designated professionals?

Summary

This introductory chapter has outlined the principles for practice that provide the foundation for an understanding of the content and context of the book. As such it has provided an opportunity to review understanding of the key definitions of child, childhood, parenting, safeguarding and child maltreatment. The chapter has also considered the professional roles and responsibilities for nurses and midwives and introduced the child protection processes and roles of lead agencies. Child maltreatment has been highlighted as a major contemporary public health issue, but seen to be amenable to a public health solution.

Safeguarding children work is challenging and emotionally demanding. Improving knowledge and the ability to practise well is important, but I know from my teaching and supervision that this may lead some to doubt their previous judgements and actions. I would like to provide reassurance that it is very likely that those who feel this way would have done the best that they could with the knowledge they had then, within the confines of their organization's prioritization of, and commitment to, safeguarding and child protection. By reading this book you will be in a better position to practise well.

Key points

- Safeguarding children applies to individuals from pre-birth to 18 years of age.
- Children's rights and child-centredness are essential to the delivery of safe, effective care and the achievement of best outcomes.

- Parents have the overriding responsibility to ensure that their children are safe; fathers need to be included in decision-making and care of their children.
- Child maltreatment is a major contemporary public health issue, but it is also open to a public health solution.

2 Prevention and early intervention

Learning outcomes

This chapter will help you to:

- Develop your knowledge and understanding of the principles of prevention and early intervention in safeguarding children and young people.
- Extend your skills in assessment to incorporate the use of the Common Assessment Framework in practice.
- Take a role as a lead professional, working with a multi-agency team around the child.
- Make a positive contribution to the safety and well-being of children through proactive practice that includes early support and family empowerment.
- Understand the Family Nurse Partnership programme.

Introduction

This chapter concerns the practice roles of nurses and midwives in prevention and early intervention in safeguarding children and young people. Three case scenarios are presented, and alongside these the rationale for nursing and midwifery actions. The cases are as follows.

- Case 1: Erin, who is 16 years old, in care, and newly pregnant. Erin is referred to the Family Nurse Partnership programme.
- Case 2: the Gordon family, who are facing difficulties in parenting their young children, receive additional support from a health visitor, including a CAF assessment.
- Case 3: Natalie, who is 15 years old and is facing pressure from her boyfriend to be more intimate, attends a school nurse 'drop in' session.

These cases are rooted in universal provision of health services – i.e. midwifery, health visiting and school nursing – although reference is also made to other key players, such as the general practitioner (GP). Throughout the chapter links are given to policy and the evidence base for practice. There are also practice questions and points, as well as suggestions for additional activities, to encourage readers to further develop the knowledge and skills required for achieving excellence in safeguarding children practice.

Case 1: Erin — support from the Family Nurse Partnership programme

Erin, who is 16 years old, and a 'looked-after young person',[1] is attending a pre-natal booking clinic run by Sarah, a midwife with a special interest in teenage pregnancy. Erin has had a series of placements since she was taken into care at the age of 11 following a sexually abusive relationship perpetrated by her mother's boyfriend, from which her mother was unable to offer her protection. Erin is attending the clinic with her current foster mother who appears to be supportive. Erin has not seen her biological father for some years and has no siblings. Recently she has stopped attending college, where she was studying for a National Vocational Qualification (NVQ) Level One in beauty therapy. Her foster mother stated that Erin had been doing well at college, and in addition to the NVQ, was retaking her mathematics General Certificate of Secondary Education (GCSE), having only narrowly missed getting a grade C the first time around. Erin is reluctant to disclose the identity of the baby's father, and says that although he is aware of the pregnancy and seems pleased by it, they are not really in a stable relationship. Sarah is concerned about Erin's preparedness for the baby and her ability to parent. She refers Erin to the Family Nurse Partnership programme.

Teenage pregnancy

Teenage pregnancy is recognized to be both a cause of, and to result in, social exclusion, poverty and inequality (TPIAG 2009). The health outcomes of the babies born to teenage mothers tend to be poorer than those born to older mothers. Teenage mothers are more likely to smoke throughout pregnancy; to have an inadequate diet; to use formula (bottle) feeds for their babies; to suffer from post-natal depression; and to be at risk of further unplanned pregnancies.

Fathers of the babies of teenage mothers tend to be teenage or in their early twenties. Young fathers are themselves more likely to have suffered child maltreatment; to be suffering from anxiety, depression or conduct disorders; to drink, smoke or misuse substances; and to have poor health and nutrition (DCSF/DH 2009). Widely-known risks for babies born to teenage parents include higher infant mortality and morbidity, prematurity, low birth weight, poor educational outcomes and greater likelihood of being unemployed in later life. There is also evidence that offspring of teenage mothers are more likely to suffer from child maltreatment when compared to their peers (Sidebotham and Heron 2006). Nevertheless, it is important to recognize that the poorer outcomes, and the greater risk of maltreatment, can also be linked to

---

[1] The term 'looked after' was introduced by the Children Act in 1989 and refers to children subject to care orders (placed into the care of local authorities by order of a court) and children accommodated by voluntary agreement of their parents. This group are increasingly referred to as 'children in care'.

the poverty and social deprivation suffered by this group and that many babies born to teenage parents do well and achieve good outcomes.

Summary of the risks and outcomes for babies born to teenage mothers

- Preterm birth
- Low birth weight
- Higher rate of morbidity and mortality
- Poorer educational outcomes
- Increased risk of suffering child maltreatment
- Greater likelihood of being unemployed in later life

The UK has the highest teenage pregnancy rate in Western Europe (OECD 2009), and the factors that contribute to this, as well as possible solutions, continue to be subject to public scrutiny and polarizing viewpoints. According to the WHO Health Evidence Network (2010), prevention of teenage pregnancy requires a raft of strategic actions. These include:

- the provision of positive and relationship-based sex education before young people become sexually active;
- access to integrated contraception and sexual health services (e.g. within schools or places that young people go to); and
- improved provision for education, employment and support for young single mothers.

Comparisons of the UK rates of teenage pregnancy are frequently made with the Netherlands, which has a more liberal relationship-based approach to sex education, more accessible contraception and sexual health services, and teenage pregnancy rates that are one-fifth of the rates in the UK. However, despite the wealth of evidence, many in the UK remain ambivalent about the mandatory provision of sex and relationship education within educational or home settings, with notable resistance from some faith-based groups.

Practice question

Reflect on your position on sex and relationship education and contraception provision to children and young people. How could this influence your practice?

Teenage pregnancy, looked-after children and young people

Looked-after children and young people are at significantly increased risk of teenage pregnancy; indeed the risk is widely quoted as being 2.5 times greater when compared with their peers. In a summary of the evidence base to support this finding, the Social Care Institute for Excellence (SCIE) concluded that this was not only because the health, education, social and economic difficulties and disadvantage were more prominent within this group, but also because they suffer from having limited access to positive adult support and yet are expected to be more independent (SCIE 2005). The SCIE review also suggested that because of educational disadvantage, including poor attainment and attendance, looked-after children and young people were unlikely to benefit from either school-based sexual health and relationship programmes, or the provision of school-based contraception and sexual health services. Drawing on consultation with young people, the review highlighted the options for greater accessibility to confidential sources of information and advice on sexual health matters, such as through media and the internet, as well as the need for provision of specialist sexual health services for this age group.

Practice point

Despite the negativity that surrounds teenage parenthood it is important for nurses and midwives to acknowledge that parenthood is a familiar 'rite of passage' and may serve to provide meaning to individuals with poor self-esteem and self-worth whose childhood has failed to allow them to achieve their potential into adulthood.

Sarah's post as a midwife with a special interest in teenage pregnancy is an example of work undertaken within the NHS to try to address young people's reported anxiety about the possible reactions of health professionals to teenage pregnancy and their additional concerns about receiving maternity care alongside older service users (DCSF/DH 2009). Sensitivity to the needs of teenage parents, and provision of bespoke services to meet these needs, can help to ensure better outcomes for their children and address the intergenerational cycle of deprivation that can ensue.

Activity

Access the *You're Welcome: Quality Criteria Self-assessment Toolkit* (DH 2009a) from the Department of Health (DH) website (www.dh.gov.uk). This toolkit has been designed to help in the planning and delivery of high-quality and 'young-person friendly' health services.

- How does your service measure up?
- What can you do to make a small and sustainable improvement?

Case 1 continued

During the booking appointment, Sarah discusses the options for Erin's care in pregnancy with her. Although Erin's foster mother is keen to contribute and be involved in the planning for the new baby, Sarah ensures that she spends some time with Erin alone. This provides an opportunity for a more sensitive discussion about her pregnancy and her relationship with the father of the baby, and to ensure that, if possible, he is able to join Erin at future appointments. Sarah also recognizes the need to consider and explore any possibility of coercion, sexual exploitation and/or sexual abuse, especially given Erin's vulnerability, disengagement from education and her initial reluctance to disclose details about the father (HM Government 2009). Once Erin is comfortable with Sarah, she will also engineer an opportunity to see her alone to address any issues of domestic (partner) violence or abuse. Sarah concludes the appointment by asking Erin where she would like to receive her care and what the best times for her future appointments might be. They discuss the use of texting to keep in touch, to help with any queries and to send new appointments. Finally, Sarah gives Erin a positive message in letting her know that she is eligible for the help and support of a practitioner from the Family Nurse Partnership programme.

The Family Nurse Partnership programme

The Family Nurse Partnership (FNP) programme is an evidence-based intensive scheme for young (typically under the age of 19) and vulnerable first-time mothers. It comprises highly-structured, scripted home visits by specially trained nurses (generally experienced health visitors and midwives) and is delivered from the pre-natal period until the child is 2 years of age. The programme, which is currently being rolled out across England and Scotland, is based on the Nurse Family Partnership programme first trialled in the USA in the late 1970s and rigorously followed up in a series of randomized controlled trials.[2] The programme focuses on outcomes across three areas, namely:

- improving outcomes in pregnancy and birth;
- enhancing child health and development; and
- improving parents' life course and economic self-sufficiency.

The structured programme of home visits focuses on health-promoting behaviours and self-efficacy skills that will improve outcomes for the mother, her child and the wider family; encourage and support access to family planning, education and opportunities to gain employment; and build supportive relationships with family members and friends. The practitioners who deliver the programme receive an intense regime of supervision.

---

[2]See www.nursefamilypartnership.org.

The key differences between FNP and the universal Healthy Child Programme (DH/DCSF 2009a) are that there is continuity of practitioner from the ante-natal period until the child's second birthday, that there are more contacts and that these are more highly structured. FNP practitioners receive additional training including the use of motivational interviewing techniques with their clients.

Evidence of the success of the programme in the USA can be summarized as:

- measurable improvements in maternal and child health;
- reduction in children's injuries, illnesses and hospital admissions;
- reduction in child maltreatment;
- improvements in school readiness and educational achievements;
- reduction in substance misuse;
- fewer subsequent pregnancies and greater intervals between births;
- less criminality by the young mothers;
- increase in fathers' involvement;
- increase in maternal employment; and
- reductions in spending on welfare.

In short, the programme demonstrates both improved outcomes for children, young people and families and cost benefits to the public purse (Olds *et al.* 1994, 1997; Eckenrode *et al.* 2010). However, because of the difference in health and social care systems in the UK, especially in the provision of universal midwifery and health visiting services (including home visits), the effects of the FNP may not be comparable to the clear indicators of success in the USA. Nevertheless, emergent evidence suggests that early adopter sites have been able to demonstrate acceptability of the programme, together with a range of encouraging outcomes including a positive impact on smoking reduction and increased rates of breast-feeding for the vulnerable young first-time mothers recruited to the programme (Barnes *et al.* 2009). Importantly, the programme is recognized to be a good example of a targeted service provision within the universally provided Healthy Child Programme (DH/DCSF 2009a) and as an intervention that has the potential to reduce health inequalities in vulnerable populations (Audit Commission 2010).

Practice question

How can targeted care within universal services be delivered to ensure that those who receive additional services gain most benefit without a sense of being stigmatized?

Erin: summary of prevention and early intervention

For Erin, if the outcomes of the FNP mirror those in the USA (albeit with the proviso given above), the baby will be more likely to be born at term, within the normal range for birth weight and to be breast-fed. The baby may also have an increased likelihood of being healthier, with a reduced possibility of suffering illness, an accident or maltreatment and may achieve greater success at school. Erin will be more likely to return to college to obtain her qualifications, gain employment and to have a longer gap before a subsequent pregnancy. The father of the baby will be more likely to be involved in their care.

Markers of good practice: the role of the midwife

Sarah, who has specialized in teenage pregnancy, understands that Erin and her baby face a risk of poor health outcomes. As a highly-skilled and knowledgeable practitioner, Sarah is able to begin to establish a positive and trusting relationship with Erin, and is able to arrange a programme of care that will meet her needs and wishes.

Sarah is able to negotiate some time to see Erin alone and will make a particular assessment of any evidence of maltreatment, including sexual exploitation. She will also assess for domestic (partner) abuse.

Case 2: the Gordon family — assessment of additional needs using the Common Assessment Framework

Marlon and Kay are the parents of two boys, Maddox, aged 22 months and Mason, aged 6 months. Kay, who has mild learning difficulties, is finding it hard to cope with the needs and demands of a baby and a toddler. Marlon often threatens to leave because he 'can't stand the babies crying'. He is currently unemployed, although had previously been working in a small local business as a storeman. Both parents smoke cigarettes, but deny the use of other substances. The family are living in a privately rented two bedroomed flat, which is difficult to heat, and often feels damp. They are concerned about the threatened cuts to housing benefit.

Kay rarely sees her mother who lives on the other side of the city. She has few friends and finds going out difficult, as Marlon is not prepared to look after the children for very long. Kay has been feeling low since the birth of Mason, who was born at 32 weeks gestation due to maternal infection. Jenny, the health visitor, is concerned about Kay's ability to meet the needs of her boys. Maddox appears to be behind in his developmental milestones and has recently missed an appointment with the community paediatrician. He often appears somewhat grubby and is usually sucking on a dummy (pacifier) while trying to hold onto Kay's legs. Mason has not yet completed his primary course of immunizations and has been somewhat poorly following an episode of bronchiolitis. There are concerns that he is failing to gain weight as expected.

Jenny, who has been offering an enhanced service with extra home visits, is concerned that without additional services the children may end up suffering from neglect of their health and developmental needs. She is also aware that both parents are trying to do their best, but are limited by their circumstances and abilities. Jenny seeks the consent of Marlon and Kay to identify their needs by undertaking an assessment using the Common Assessment Framework (CAF).

The Common Assessment Framework

The CAF is a process of shared holistic assessment and planning that is linked to the early identification of needs in families who may require additional services. It is part of a set of materials for practitioners and their managers that are designed to support the implementation of the *Every Child Matters* policy (DfES 2004) and is an important element of the move towards integrated delivery of front line services (CWDC 2009). In theory, any 'children's workforce' professional should be able to undertake a CAF, and those working most closely with the child or young person are ideally placed to do so. In practice this means that professionals such as health visitors or school nurses are at the forefront of using this tool to empower children, young people and their families to identify areas of need, potential solutions and sources of help.

'It can be helpful to consider the needs of families and the services provided to them as part of a continuum from services that all families receive to specialist services for those with complex needs, including those in need of protection. The majority of children, young people and families will receive universal services. These are essentially those provided by health services, early years settings and schools e.g. general practitioner services, midwifery, health visiting and school nursing as detailed in the *Healthy Child Programme* DH, DCSF 2009a & b). A smaller number of children will have some additional needs over and above universal provision (e.g. a referral to speech therapy or additional learning support). However, only a minority will require co-ordinated, integrated support for more complex needs involving professionals from different agencies and organisations (e.g. missing education, complex disability, multiple deprivation, impact of parental difficulties). Statutory child protection proceedings would apply to a small minority of families at the extreme of the continuum.'

In representing the dynamic and changing nature of needs within families it is important to note that movement takes place across the continuum of need; however, the aim is always to intervene early to support movement towards minimal intervention in family life and universal provision of services. It is also important to recognise that where there are additional needs these can be met by one practitioner. However, where the needs and service provision is more complex, an involved practitioner will take on a role as 'Lead Professional' to act as a single point of contact for the family. Nurses and midwives from a range of specialities may take on this role; equally it may be more applicable for another professional e.g. from the Youth Offending Team or Education Welfare services to do so.

The Lead Professional ensures that the child or young person and their family receive appropriate and timely interventions. This includes seeing that these are delivered and reviewed in a planned way that reduces the possibility of duplication or overlap. Where others need to be involved, a Team Around the Child (TAC) meeting, involving the family and professionals will help to ensure good join-up of services.

If a CAF has been completed it is a useful adjunct to a referral to children's social care services (or indeed any other service). However, in my experience, there appears to be some confusion in practice as to expectations of CAF as part of the referral process. *Working Together* is clear that 'Undertaking a CAF is not a prerequisite for making a referral' (HM Government 2010: 139).

The design of the CAF is based on the domains of the *Framework for the Assessment for the of Children in Need and their Families* (DH 2000):

- the development of the infant, child or young person (including unborn babies);
- the parents and carers; and
- the family and environment.

The CAF assessment is designed to help professionals work with families to identify their strengths and needs according to criteria highlighted within the three domains. The aim of the CAF is to ensure early help and support and to prevent situations from escalating to a higher tier of need. It also helps to ensure that families are not subject to multiple assessments and that where more than one agency are working with a family there is a joined-up approach.

Table 2.1 outlines the areas that are assessed within a CAF.

The CAF is now electronically-enabled (i.e. available as an online tool) to ensure that the assessment, planning and review elements are appropriately shared and updated. 'E-enablement' can also help the strategic planning of services by making it easier to analyse the demographics of families who have had a CAF.

Table 2.1 CAF domains

Child	Parent and carer	Family and environment
• General health • Physical, emotional and social development • Behaviour • Self-esteem and learning	• Basic care • Safety and protection • Emotional warmth • Stability • Guidance • Boundaries and stimulation	• Family history, functioning and well-being • The wider family • Housing • Employment and finance • Social and community resources

Activity

Go to www.cwdcouncil.org.uk/caf to access and complete a CAF for the Gordon family.

A qualitative study to evaluate the impact of CAF on the outcomes for children, young people and their families suggests that there is some evidence to show improvements in children's physical and emotional health, financial support and housing (Easton *et al.* 2010). Participants in the study included children, young people and their families as well as practitioners from the children's workforce. Midwives, health visitors and school nurses were among those drawn from health agencies. In addition to the indications of better outcomes for children, the study also noted improved integrated working and trust between agencies. However, the authors concluded that more work was needed to ensure that the outcomes achieved were sustainable.

Case 2 continued

The evidence suggests that the children of parents with a learning disability may be more likely to have developmental delay and that any delay may be compounded by a potential for lack of stimulation within their environment (Gaw 2000). Although Kay's learning disability is thought to be mild, it is important that those providing care to the family are sensitive and appreciate that the impact of detailed assessment may add to a common fear within this group that their children may be removed from their care. Before starting the assessment Jenny seeks consent, ensuring that Kay and Marlon understand the nature of the CAF and how the information that is shared may be stored and used. She also provides reassurance that the process will help to identify where parenting is going well, in addition to discovering what else may be needed to ensure that the boys are able to achieve their health and developmental potential.

Jenny thinks that at the current time the needs of the family can be met through some targeted support and monitoring provided by the health visiting team and children's centre. The CAF action plan includes the following.

For the parents:

- to attend Maddox's appointment with the paediatrician to assess for developmental delay;
- to agree to a referral for Maddox to attend the speech and language therapy service;
- to take Mason to the GP to complete his schedule of immunizations;
- to attend the Thursday drop-in parent and toddler group; a volunteer from the group will come and meet the family at home to befriend Kay;

- for Kay to see the GP to discuss post-natal depression;
- for Marlon and Kay to address their family planning needs;
- for Marlon and Kay to seek help from the local smoke-stop service; if they continue to smoke they will do so on the balcony to the flat, and not in front of the children.

For the health visiting team:

- the health visitor to make an application to an early years scheme that supports nursery placements for vulnerable 2-year-olds;
- the nursery nurse to undertake a programme of weekly visits to model suitable play activities for both boys;
- the health visitor to arrange an invitation for the parents to attend a parenting group at the centre;
- the health visitor to write to the local housing officer to support a move into more suitable accommodation for the family.

The Gordon family: summary of prevention and early intervention

The decision to undertake the CAF was based on the evidence that the children had unmet health and developmental needs and the understanding that early intervention may help to avoid issues reaching crisis point. Plans to meet the additional needs were put in place. The situation will be reviewed in due course; if there is evidence that unmet needs remain, additional services may be required. Additional services may be offered within a programme of integrated support, with the convening of a TAC meeting and identification of a lead professional (possibly the health visitor). However, if concerns about the neglect of the two children continue or escalate, then it will be necessary to refer the case to children's social care services.

Markers of good practice: the role of the health visitor

Despite offering an enhanced service, Jenny recognizes that the Gordon family have a number of unmet needs that are impacting on the health and development of the children. With consent from the parents, a CAF is completed. This recognizes some strengths within the family, but also enables the completion of an action plan to ensure that needs are addressed.

While feeling sympathy for the parents, Jenny will ensure that her focus remains on the 'daily lived experience' of the children and will escalate her concerns to children's social care, if necessary.

Case 3: Natalie — prevention and support from the school nursing service

Natalie is a quiet and studious 15-year-old who has recently become involved with Hunter, a mature student at the nearby university. Her father is a civil engineer and her mother works part-time at a local nursery school. She has a younger brother who is due to join her at her secondary school the following academic year. Natalie is concerned that her family would disapprove of her friendship with Hunter, and has begun to meet him secretly, while telling her parents that she is working in the library after school. Hunter has had previous relationships and is putting pressure on Natalie to be more intimate. She is aware that other students in her class are involved in sexual relationships with their partners, and is anxious that she is not seen to be 'swot' with no life outside her studies. Natalie believes that if she does not agree to sleep with Hunter he will end their relationship. She is becoming increasingly anxious and withdrawn. At a recent parents' evening her form tutor expressed concern that she seemed unhappy and that her grades had slipped over the previous term. In an effort to continue the relationship, Natalie arranges to stay overnight at the halls of residence, telling her parents that she is having a 'sleep-over' at her best friend's house. Knowing that the school nurse, Cynthia, is able to provide contraception and sexual health advice, Natalie decides to attend a lunch-time drop-in session.

Underage sexual activity

In the UK the 'age of consent' is 16 years. Sexual activity before this age could be considered to be unlawful[3] although it is widely recognized that legal action is unlikely for consensual sex of those aged 13 years or over with a partner within their age group. The same rules apply whether the activity is heterosexual or homosexual. Prosecution will be more likely the larger the age gap, or where there is an imbalance of power, or an individual has a position of trust or authority (e.g. a health professional or teacher).

Working Together (HM Government 2010) aligns the issue of sexual activity in young people with the safeguarding children arena. The guidance provides an excellent framework for directing and supporting practice for school nurses, others working in contraception and sexual health services, maternity services, emergency departments, walk-in centres and general practice.

Broadly speaking the guidance recognizes that children under the age of 13 are not capable of consenting to sexual activity and that there is a 'presumption' that the case will be referred to children's social care services (HM Government 2010: 141). Where a young person is aged 13–15 years, the guidance suggests that consideration should be made as to whether there should be

---

[3]Sexual Offences Act 2003.

a discussion with children's social care. A checklist to help in decision-making in relation to whether the sexual activity means that the young person is at risk of, or suffering, significant harm is provided. This includes the need to assess the level of maturity and understanding of the young person, an age imbalance and other factors which may suggest abuse of power.

In addition to guidance on 'underage' sexual activity, *Working Together* also notes that sexual activity involving a 16- or 17-year-old may still involve harm or the likelihood of harm being suffered, and that a sexual relationship would be an offence if a person held a position of trust or authority.

Practice question

Access the *Working Together* guidance and read the section on underage sexual activity: www.workingtogetheronline.co.uk/chapter_five.html. What advice and support would you give to a 15-year-old seeking contraception and sexual health advice in the following circumstances?

- Their partner was 18 years of age
- Their partner was 28 years of age
- They were reluctant to disclose details of their partner
- They appeared to have a learning difficulty
- They were accompanied by an older adult who didn't disclose their relationship with the young person
- They looked younger than their stated 15 years
- They said they were 'coming for a friend'
- They disclosed use of alcohol and/or other substances

Case 3 continued

At 15 Natalie believes that she is in a minority within her peer group because she is still a virgin. However, evidence reported by Godeau *et al.* (2008), who studied the sexual activity and contraceptive use of just under 34,000 15-year-olds in 24 countries, found that in England 39.9 per cent of girls reported that they had had sexual intercourse (interestingly the figure for the Netherlands was 20.5 per cent). Hunter is 25 years old.

Practice question

Should Cynthia, the school nurse, be considering sharing information with children's social care and/or the police?

School nurses working in 'drop-in' sessions with children and young people will be working within the remit of the professional code (NMC 2008). In establishing a rapport, it will be important for Cynthia to ensure that Natalie understands the issues in relation to consent and confidentiality. Specific guidance on school nursing is helpful to all parties:

> Children and young people have the right to a confidential school health service, and as a result information shared between a child or young person and a school nurse will not necessarily be shared with a school. However, where children are identified as at risk of harm it is expected that information will be shared appropriately according to local child protection policy.
>
> (DH/DfES 2006: 22–3)

Cynthia considers that Natalie is presenting as a vulnerable young person who is at risk of harm. While letting Natalie know that she has been sensible to 'drop in' to discuss contraception, she shares her concerns that Hunter is considerably older than she is and that she may be being coerced into a sexual relationship before she is ready. Cynthia also explains that the secret nature of their relationship is particularly worrying and adds that because Natalie (and others) may be at risk from Hunter's predatory behaviour she would like to share information about him with children's social care and the police. Cynthia also encourages Natalie to be more open with her parents, while assuring her of the confidentiality of the health aspects of the consultation, in particular that information will not be shared with her parents or the school. Finally, she advises Natalie that the majority of 15-year-olds are unlikely to be engaging in sexual activity, whatever her classmates say. Natalie is visibly relieved.

Natalie: summary of prevention and early intervention

Underage sexual activity is unlawful and can be a serious cause of concern. Even where it is consensual there may be 'serious consequences to the welfare of the young person' (HM Government 2010: 142), including unplanned pregnancy and sexually-transmitted disease. Where there is a clear imbalance of age or power this needs to be considered as 'sexual exploitation' with a clear risk of significant harm to a young person or other young people (see Chapter 5). Information may need to be shared with statutory agencies (i.e. children's social care and/or the police) and this should be explained to the young person, and where possible, their consent gained to do so. The actions of the school nurse will protect Natalie's well-being and potentially add to intelligence about an individual who poses a threat to young girls.

Markers of good practice: the role of the school nurse

Cynthia runs a confidential 'drop in' session to support the health needs of young people in a place and at a time to suit them. The aim is to promote health and well-being, especially in relation to physical, emotional and sexual health.

While acknowledging the step that Natalie has made in consulting with her as a sign of maturity, Cynthia has also recognized her vulnerability within a relationship which is marked by secrecy and an imbalance of power.

Cynthia seeks supervision and support from the named nurse safeguarding children (see Chapter 1). She then contacts the local children's social care department and the police.

Cynthia completes clear, contemporaneous records of her decision-making and actions (NMC 2009b).

Summary

This chapter has applied the principles of prevention and early intervention in safeguarding children to nursing and midwifery practice. This has included exploring the notion of targeting services within a universal service (i.e. the FNP, enhanced health visiting and proactive school nursing) and has demonstrated the importance of the assessment skills of the practitioners. Through considering Cynthia's actions, the chapter has also demonstrated that the actions of nurses and midwives can have a significant impact on the wider health and safety of children and young people. Some prevention and early intervention will take place at a 'single agency' level. However, much of what can be achieved is also reliant on working in an integrated way with others, with the welfare of the child, young person and their family always at the centre. Working with others to safeguard and promote the welfare of children and young people will be explored in more detail in the remaining chapters.

Key points

- Midwives, health visitors and school nurses have a range of opportunities to contribute to the prevention and early identification of child abuse and neglect.
- The FNP may confer a range of improved outcomes for the most vulnerable families, including a reduction in child maltreatment.

- The CAF process provides a framework to assess strengths and needs within a family and to ensure timely support.
- Those providing contraception and sexual health services need to practise within the framework of legislation and guidance. This will include supporting children and young people's safety, as well as their health.

3 Physical abuse

Learning outcomes

This chapter will help you to:

- Understand the features of physical abuse as a form of child maltreatment.
- Identify indicators that may be associated with physical abuse, including fabricated and induced illness.
- Outline the key components of nursing assessment, paediatric examination and investigations in cases of possible physical abuse.
- Understand the process for referral of cases of suspected child maltreatment to the lead statutory agencies (children's social care and/or the police) and the purpose of the strategy discussion.
- Appreciate the role and functions of the named nurse safeguarding children and the local authority social worker.

Introduction

This chapter considers physical abuse as a form of child maltreatment. Physical abuse can present in many different ways, and may be difficult to distinguish from accidental injuries. This chapter does not aim to be inclusive of all possible presentations. However, what it does aim to do is develop nurses' and midwives' understanding of how this form of child maltreatment may present; the factors that may help to inform its identification and referral; and what the nursing actions should be. The aim is to ensure that children and young people are safeguarded and protected from further harm in a timely and appropriate way. We begin by providing a brief overview of the features of physical abuse.

Drawing on the statutory guidance we define what is meant by 'physical abuse' and outline some of the key indicators of concern. Three case scenarios are presented, together with the nursing actions. The cases are as follows:

- Case 1: Kayla, aged 10 weeks, who is visiting the practice nurse for her first immunization. A bruise is noted.

- Case 2: Ethan, aged 14 months, who has attended the emergency department with two small burns on his hand; he is noticed to be somewhat withdrawn.
- Case 3: Naimah, a 6-year-old, who has been admitted to a children's hospital for investigations of chronic diarrhoea.

The cases are fictitious, but based on real events. As in the previous chapter, reference is made to safeguarding children policy, as well as the underpinning evidence for practice. The chapter concludes by summarizing key practice points to help to reinforce knowledge and best practice.

Physical abuse

The definitions provided in *Working Together* for the purposes of statutory child protection proceedings and planning are a useful starting point in helping those working with children, young people and their families to understand child maltreatment and its presenting features (HM Government 2010). Here, four 'categories' of maltreatment are referred to: physical abuse, emotional abuse, sexual abuse and neglect. Physical abuse is described as involving: 'hitting, shaking, throwing, poisoning, burning or scalding, drowning, suffocating or otherwise causing physical harm to a child. Physical harm may also be caused when a parent or carer fabricates the symptoms of, or deliberately induces, illness in a child' (HM Government 2010: 38).

Children and young people who become subject to a child protection plan in one of the four categories are considered to have unresolved safeguarding children issues and remain at risk of significant harm. The percentage of children who are subject to a child protection plan because of physical abuse has accounted for some 15 per cent of the total number with such a plan in recent years; although this in itself is not indicative of the incidence or prevalence of this type of abuse.[1] The issue of the legality of physical punishment blurs the boundaries between what some would consider acceptable treatment of children, and others abusive (Polnay *et al.* 2007). However, the suggestion that as many as 7 per cent of all children may suffer from serious physical abuse during their childhood (Cawson *et al.* 2000) is widely quoted within the field.

At the severe end of the spectrum, physical abuse can lead to permanent disability or death. Infants are particularly at risk. The National Society for the Prevention of Cruelty to Children (NSPCC) provides a helpful explanation of how child maltreatment death statistics are gathered. The NSPCC has updated the widely reported previous estimates of one to two child fatalities per week (in England and Wales) by including the reviews of the serious childcare incidents that are reported to the Office for Standards in Education (Ofsted). As a result of this work, the NSPCC now suggests that up to four children die

---

[1] Annual child protection statistics for the UK are available from: www.statistics.gov.uk/hub/children-education-skills/children-and-early-years-education/child-safety-and-well-being.

as a result of maltreatment each week.[2] While such tragedies may occur in circumstances where there are no apparent prior indicators of maltreatment, a history of escalating concerns about physical injuries, and other indicators of abuse, is a feature of many serious case reviews, albeit with the benefit of hindsight.

Identification of non-accidental (or 'intentional' or 'inflicted') injuries or patterns of injuries is thus an important professional role and responsibility for nurses, midwives, health visitors and others in contact with children and their families. The box below contains extracts from the serious case review into the circumstances leading up to the death of Peter Connelly ('Baby Peter'). The injuries that are described are unusual for a baby and suggestive of non-accidental injury.

Extracts from *Serious Case Review: Baby Peter*

[Peter's mother] said she did not know when or how the swelling on Peter's forehead had occurred. She attributed the other bruises to him climbing and falling and bruising easily, as well as slapping his body in play ... The body map made at the time shows extensive bruising to his buttocks and other bruises to his face and chest, including the swelling to his forehead which had triggered the referral from the GP ... No adult had given any explanation of how Peter had sustained these injuries and who was with him when he sustained them. This was very concerning for a nine month old baby.

(Haringey Safeguarding Children Board 2009: 7–8)

Recognizing physical abuse

The Royal College of Paediatrics and Child Health (RCPCH) notes that while there are 'few diagnostic signs' of physical abuse (RCPCH 2006: 17) there are a number of presenting features that may suggest that a child has been deliberately harmed. These include:

- a history of the injury that is vague or inconsistent (including differing accounts from each parent);
- a report of an unwitnessed event (especially in infants and young children);
- a description of events that does not seem to explain the injury or fit with the child's developmental abilities;
- frequent presentations to emergency departments and/or minor injury units;
- more than one injury, or a pattern of injuries;

---

[2]See www.nspcc.org.uk/Inform/research/Briefings/child_killings_in_england_and_wales_wda67213.html.

- a delay in presenting for treatment;
- poor interaction between parents and the child.

Practice point

Children who are developmentally able should be encouraged and supported to provide their own history for a presenting injury. They should also be given an opportunity during a consultation to be seen without the accompanying parent or carer – the approach should always aim to be 'child-centred'.

The following case scenarios describe three different presentations of physical child abuse. Links are made to the evidence base for practice and to statutory guidance. In each case the actions of the nurse are described in terms of best practice.

Case 1: Kayla – an infant with bruising

Kayla, who is 10 weeks old, is attending an appointment with the practice nurse, Laurel, to have her first immunization. She is the first baby of Lucie and Mark, who have been together for a year or so in a somewhat volatile relationship. Kayla is a small baby, having been born at term, but with a birth weight of 2,479 grams. She is fed on infant formula milk and has just begun to smile. As she prepares to give the vaccine, Laurel notices a small fresh bruise on Kayla's upper thigh. Lucie is unable to provide an explanation for the bruise, and in undertaking a further assessment of the baby, Laurel finds a further bruise on Kayla's back.

Practice point

Evidence from a robust controlled study suggests that breast-feeding may have a protective effect against maternally perpetrated child maltreatment (Strathearn et al. 2009). This is thought to be due to the release of oxytocin which in turn is associated with mood elevation and reduction in stress in breast-feeding women.

Bruising

Bruising is the most common presentation of physical abuse (NCCWCH 2009). However, accidental bruising in children is also very common, and it is thus important that nurses and midwives have an appreciation of presentations of bruising that may be indicative of physical abuse. The NCCWCH clinical guidelines are particularly helpful, and conclude that where there is bruising in

Table 3.1 Bruising

Non-accidental bruising	Accidental bruising
• Unexplained/no history given	• Explanation/history provided
• Bruising in a child who is not independently mobile	• More common in summer months
	• Bruising in an independently mobile child
• Bruises on any non-bony part of the face or body including eyes, ears, cheeks, upper arm, outer thigh and buttocks	• Bruises on the knees, shins, elbows, forehead, nose, centre of chin, back of head
• Bruises on the neck that look like attempted strangulation	
• Bruising in the shape of a hand, ligature, stick, teeth marks, grip, implement	
• Multiple bruises or clustering of bruises	

Source: adapted from NCCWH (2009) and WCPSRG/NSPCC (2009a)

babies and children who are not independently mobile, and no clear history of an accidental cause is given, practitioners should suspect non-accidental injury (i.e. maltreatment). In comparison, independently mobile children and young people will sustain accidental bruising in everyday activities – for example, in play and sporting activities. Table 3.1 compares some key features of accidental and non-accidental bruising.

Although guidelines as to how to 'age' a bruise have been published in the past, the evidence for this is not conclusive and current advice is that it should not be attempted.

Case 1 continued

The presence of any injury in an infant is concerning and may suggest more serious injury, including the possibility of a brain or abdominal injury (RCPCH 2006). Kayla is only 10 weeks old. The next step for Laurel, the practice nurse, is to raise her concerns with Lucie and to explain that Kayla will need to be seen by a paediatrician and that a referral to the local authority children's social care service will be made. A body map[3] may be used to indicate the position of the bruises.

In some areas the paediatrician will see the child prior to the referral to children's social care and in others this will be arranged in conjunction with children's social care (according to local policy and procedures). Referrals to children's social care are normally made by telephone in the first instance and followed up in writing within 48 hours, usually on an inter-agency referral form designed for this purpose. Lucie, Kayla's mother, should be fully informed

---

[3]See RCPCH (2006: Appendix 13).

about the referral to children's social care, unless doing so would place Kayla at increased risk of harm. The practice nurse will need to carefully document her findings and actions, including any explanation for the injury that is offered by Lucie. In a very small minority of cases there will be a medical explanation for the bruising.

Raising the possibility that an infant or child may have been deliberately harmed is challenging. However, the duty of care is first and foremost to the child, who is totally dependent on others to recognize the possibility of maltreatment. Every practice situation calls for communication on an individualized basis. Laurel should both seek to find an explanation for the bruises and be clear that bruising in a small baby is unusual and can indicate that *someone* may have harmed Kayla. She will explain that because of this Kayla will need to be seen by a paediatrician and be referred to children's social care.

It is also good practice to inform the GP of the situation at the earliest opportunity. However, the practice nurse is independently professionally accountable for her actions (NMC 2008). The practice has a responsibility to ensure that Kayla is taken for further assessment and to provide relevant details to those making child protection enquiries. Finally, the practice nurse should ensure that the health visiting service is made aware of the referral, according to local arrangements for primary care liaison.

Practice point

There should also be concern about the welfare of Kayla's mother, Lucie, as domestic violence and abuse is indicated. Children living with domestic abuse are at a notably increased risk of physical abuse and other forms of child maltreatment (Humphreys and Stanley 2006).

Referral to children's social care

Further details of the process of referral to children's social care can be found in *Working Together*, Chapter 5 (HM Government 2010) and Local Safeguarding Children Board (LSCB) inter-agency procedures. As we noted in Chapter 1, each health care organization should also have its own safeguarding children policy and procedures, including details of how to contact safeguarding leads for advice and support in the identification and referral of concerns about possible child maltreatment. When a referral has been made, children's social care will liaise with the police, who will have a responsibility to progress any criminal investigation arising from safeguarding children concerns.

The sharing of information is an important part of the process and information from the GP and the health visitor will provide context for the child protection enquiries. Support and advice for health professionals who are concerned that a child has been abused or who need help with progressing a referral to children's social care can be obtained from named or designated health professionals. The police should be notified of any situations that may further endanger the child, for example parental refusal to comply with the requirements for their child to be seen. The Children Act 1989 has a provision known as 'police protection' (Section 46) that allows a police officer to either move a child to a place of safety or prevent a child being taken from a place of safety. Police protection can last for up to 72 hours.

Case 1 continued

Kayla will have a comprehensive paediatric assessment and medical examination. As she has presented with bruising this will include investigations to exclude the possibility of bleeding disorders or meningococcal septicaemia, which may look like bruising. The paediatrician will also take a full family and social history, and document the findings carefully. This will include taking details of who has had care of Kayla (which will also be part of the police and social care enquiries). The bruises will be recorded on a body map and may be photographed by a medical or forensic photographer (RCPCH 2006).

Kayla is a small baby, and the assessment will include a measurement of her current weight and plotting of previous known weights, including her birth weight, on a 'centile chart'. Previous weights (and other health details) should be available in the 'parent-held child health record' (widely known as the 'red book'). Lucie will be asked to share this record with the professionals undertaking the assessment.

Children who suffer physical abuse may also show signs of neglect. A key indicator of neglect is a failure of growth along expected centiles (see Chapter 6). Kayla is reported to have *just* started to smile. This is later than expected (normally 6 weeks of age) and may suggest developmental delay (Sheridan *et al.* 2008).

Practice point

Those who provide care to infants, children and young people should be familiar with key developmental milestones. Child maltreatment is one of the many causes of developmental delay in children (Polnay *et al.* 2007).

In cases of suspected physical abuse of infants under the age of 12 months, a skeletal survey will normally be undertaken to see if fractures are also present. According to NCCWCH (2009) guidelines, non-accidental fractures are more common in infants and toddlers, and may also be 'occult' – i.e. not clinically evident on physical examination. Some fractures, especially metaphyseal or rib fractures, can occur without bruising (WCPSRG/NSPCC 2009a). The skeletal survey provides a standard series of images that enable the whole skeleton to be visualized (Royal College of Radiologists (RCPCH) 2008). As with the blood tests, it is important that Lucie and Mark (assuming Mark has parental responsibility – see Chapter 1) are informed of the rationale for undertaking this investigation, which is essentially to exclude the presence of disease or other injuries.

A further key concern is the possibility that Kayla may have sustained a non-accidental head injury. Non-accidental head injury is the commonest cause of death in physical child abuse and most commonly presents in infants younger than 6 months of age. Given the presentation of bruising in a young baby, neuroimaging in the form of a computerized tomography (CT) scan may be ordered (RCPCH 2006). There is more discussion about non-accidental head injury in one of the case scenarios described in Chapter 7.

Possible investigations for suspected non-accidental injury

- Full blood count and clotting studies
- Skeletal survey
- CT scan
- Forensic photography

Kayla: summary of concerns

Kayla was noted by the practice nurse to have bruising to her upper thigh and back. Bruising in an infant is highly indicative of physical maltreatment and may indicate a risk for more serious injury. The practice nurse, seeing Kayla for a routine immunization, took action to address her concerns with the mother and to make a referral for further paediatric assessment and enquiries by children's social care.

Markers of good practice: the role of the practice nurse

As a practitioner who has responsibility for seeing infants and children for care, including immunizations, Laurel is familiar with child care and development and has a good understanding of indicators of possible child maltreatment.

Laurel is aware that bruising in an infant who is not independently mobile is indicative of physical child abuse, especially in the absence of an explanation.

Laurel correctly refers the case to children's social care, informs the GP of her concerns, and explains to the child's mother that further paediatric assessment and examination will be required. She will follow up her telephone referral to social care in writing, and liaise with the health visitor.

Laurel completes clear, contemporaneous records of the events and her actions (NMC 2009b).

Case 2: Ethan — a toddler with burns

Ethan, aged 14 months, is taken to the emergency department by his father, who has care of him during alternate weekends and for one night each week. Ethan has two blistered areas on his hands, said to be caused by offering him food that had been reheated in the microwave.[4] One of the areas looks as though it is infected. Ethan has been to the emergency department on four previous occasions and, as had been noted on the most recent visit, he appears to be somewhat withdrawn and quiet. Michael, an emergency nurse practitioner, is allocated to care for Ethan and his father.

Thermal injuries

According to the WCPSRG/NSPCC (2008) most burns and scalds are accidental, with approximately 10 per cent of burns seen in children admitted to specialist burns units thought to be a result of an intentional (non-accidental) injury. However, neglect to provide for the safety of a child is an important contributory factor in many additional cases, and this would include failure to protect a child from sunburn. Burns are painful, potentially lethal, and can cause lifelong scarring and psychological damage (NCCWCH 2009).

Safety advice: prevention of burns and scalds in children

- Set the thermostat on hot water systems to a maximum of 50°C
- Ensure safety when ironing, cooking and making hot drinks
- Remove cigarette lighters and matches from children's reach
- Provide additional protection from the sun for babies and young children

---

As with bruising there are some features or patterns of thermal injury that may raise suspicion as to the possibility of child physical abuse. These include (NCCWCH 2009: 31–2):

- the presence of upper limit or symmetrical scalds on the extremities;
- glove or stocking pattern of injury;

---

[4] The suitability of a microwave for heating baby and toddler food and drinks remains open to debate, however, it is common practice and appropriate advice should be given about 'hot spots' and testing food.

- an isolated scald on the buttocks, perineum or lower extremities;
- a scald that is uniform in depth, where flexures are spared or, in the case of immersion;
- co-existing other injuries, including fractures;
- previous burn injury;
- burns on a not independently mobile child;
- burns or scalds that are in the shape of an implement.

In any presentation of physical injury it is important to also consider late presentation, whether the history is compatible with the explanation given, the general appearance of the child, previous medical and social history and current family and social circumstances. A lack of parental concern, or the presentation of the child by an unrelated adult are important indicators of the possibility of non-accidental injury.

Practice point

Each year up to 50 per cent of infants and 25 per cent of older children present to an emergency department or urgent care centre. Children account for some 25 per cent of all emergency department attendances. Clinical staff working in these areas need to be competent in caring for children and young people. This will include having skills in child development, communication with children and young people, and child protection (Association of Paediatric Emergency Medicine et al. 2007; NHS Institute for Innovation and Improvement 2008; RCPCH/RCN 2010).

Case 2 continued

Ethan and his father will be seen promptly for triage and treatment, including pain relief as appropriate. Registration details will include noting who the health visitor is (or which health visiting team is responsible for Ethan's care) and contact may be made directly with the liaison health visitor according to local protocols to ensure rapid exchange of health information. Michael, the emergency nurse practitioner, will also note the relationship of the accompanying adult(s) (Association of Paediatric Emergency Medicine et al. 2007). Michael will access the details of previous attendances at the emergency department (and ask about attendance at other centres, for example minor injury/walk-in facilities). He will make a full health assessment (including body weight), establish a developmental and social history and conduct an examination for the presence of other injuries. He will also ensure that a check has been undertaken to see if Ethan is currently subject to a child protection plan.

In respect of this presentation Michael will ask for details of the timing and mechanism of the injury and cross-check with any explanation that has been given to colleagues in triage. Findings will be recorded, and a body map completed. Michael will seek the opinion of a senior medical practitioner, either a paediatrician or a senior doctor in emergency medicine. The most concerning aspect of this presentation is the fact that both hands are blistered. At 14 months of age Ethan will be keen to try out his sense of touch and be developing his fine motor movements and reach. He will also be attempting to feed himself. However, he would be unlikely to place *both* hands in hot food.

Practice point

Benger and McCabe (2001) developed a 'reminder checklist' for assessment of burns and scalds in pre-school children in the emergency department. The checklist asks practitioners to record:

- Any unexpected delay? Yes*/No
- History consistent and compatible? Yes/No*
- Any unexplained injuries? Yes*/No
- Behaviour/interaction appropriate? Yes/No*

Any response that is marked * means that the child should be seen by a senior medic.

It is likely that Ethan will be admitted to the children's ward. Good practice dictates that children should not be discharged while concerns remain about their safety or well-being (Laming 2009). A referral will be made to children's social care, as per Kayla's case (Case 1). Because of the concerns that this is a non-accidental injury, a social worker will convene and lead a formal strategy discussion.

Strategy discussions

A strategy discussion, led by children's social care and involving senior practitioners from the police, health staff and other relevant colleagues should be convened whenever there is 'reasonable cause to suspect that a child is suffering, or is likely to suffer significant harm' (HM Government 2010: 152). The discussion will normally be held within one working day of a concern coming to light. In an emergency a discussion can be held over the telephone, although this can limit the contribution of the participants and the rich discussion that results from a face-to-face meeting. Where a child is in hospital it is expected that the medical consultant in charge of the child's care attends, along with a senior member of the ward's nursing team. Where a child has needed specialist care (e.g. from an orthopaedic team), then their involvement may also be key. In practice this might mean a paediatrician reporting on their behalf. If a parent is experiencing problems such as domestic violence, substance misuse or mental health problems, then a professional from one of the supporting services may also be involved.

Practice point

Nurses, midwives and health visitors have an important role in contributing to strategy discussions. This will include providing valuable history and context, including child care and developmental progress and any specific health needs. Where a child is an inpatient, ward staff are well placed to comment on interactions between children and their parents and carers. Nursing and midwifery staff should be supported at strategy discussions by a safeguarding children specialist such as a named nurse.

The purpose of the strategy discussion is to:

- share information about the nature and context of the concerns;
- agree the timing and conduct of any criminal investigation;
- make a decision on the need to undertake child protection enquiries;
- ensure the immediate safety of the child (and any other children in the family); and
- discuss what information will be shared with the family (unless to do so would increase the risk to the child or other children or jeopardize any criminal investigations).

Those contributing to the strategy discussion will need to ensure that information-sharing and decision-making reflects the best interests of the child, and that the outcome of the meeting includes plans to ascertain their wishes and feelings.

Ethan: summary of concerns

Ethan has sustained burns to both hands representing a symmetrical injury to extremities that is not consistent with developmental expectations. Furthermore, the fact that one of the burns looks infected may suggest a delay in presentation. The fact that Ethan has previous attendances at the emergency department, as well as his demeanour, add to concerns. This presentation needs to be treated as a child protection concern.

Markers of good practice: the role of the emergency nurse practitioner

Children and young people represent approximately one quarter of all attendances in the emergency department, and it is thus important that those practising in this setting are competent in the delivery of care. If a nurse working in an area that treats children does not hold a children's nursing qualification they should work under the supervision and guidance of a registered nurse (child), until they are deemed competent in the delivery of care to children.

As an emergency nurse practitioner, Michael is responsible for the care and assessment of a number of children and young people each day. His experience has informed his expertise in recognizing a sick child – i.e. his awareness of developmental milestones and the range of behaviours and interactions between children, young people and their parents.

Michael undertakes a comprehensive assessment of Ethan. This includes a full, detailed history and examination. He also checks Ethan's child protection status, and re-reviews details of the previous attendances.

Michael considers that there had been some delay in the presentation of Ethan, and is also concerned about the child's demeanour and senses a wariness between Ethan and his father.

Michael is also of the opinion that the history of the injury is incompatible with the findings. He discusses his assessment and concerns about possible maltreatment with his senior and a paediatric opinion is sought.

Michael will complete a notification form for the attention of the liaison health visitor (with details of the attendance). He will also complete the written referral to children's social care and attend the strategy discussion.

Michael completes clear, contemporaneous record of the events and his actions.

Case 3: Naimah — a 6-year-old in hospital

The final scenario in this chapter concerns the special challenges of caring for a child and family where there are concerns that indicate that the child is presenting within the 'spectrum' (RCPCH 2009) of illness behaviour that may indicate fabricated or induced illness (FII). Naimah, who is 6 years old, has been admitted to a ward in a specialist children's hospital. This is her fourth admission, and as before she is accompanied by her mother who wishes to be resident. Naimah is a bright girl, but her education is suffering due to frequent absences from the classroom. Naimah's parents are divorced and she is their only child. Her father works abroad in the oil industry, and her mother, Ariana, is a full-time mother and housewife, who previously completed two years of an advanced diploma in nursing (adult branch), failing to progress to the final year because of her own ill health.

Naimah has been admitted because of her mother's continuing concerns about her abdominal pain and loose stools, reporting that sometimes she has up to six episodes of diarrhoea in a day. A number of investigations have already been performed including tests to rule out infection and coeliac disease. Naimah has also been treated with an antispasmodic medication and several courses of metronidazole. To date no diagnosis has been confirmed. Naimah's mother is pleased to recognize Sally, the ward sister, whom she considers empathetic and caring.

Naimah was born at 32 weeks gestation, her mother – who describes 'poor personal health' – having previously suffered a number of miscarriages. As a baby Naimah was reported to have lactose intolerance and required special infant formula feeds. As a toddler she was presented to her GP with reports of skin allergies. This proved difficult to treat and Ariana sought further advice from a number of complementary medicine practitioners, including several consultations with a herbalist.

Sally reviews the records and admits Naimah to the ward. Since she knew that Naimah was returning for more investigations, Sally has expressed disquiet about the possibility of FII. She feels that Naimah is essentially a well child, whose frequent presentations for health care and investigations are concerning. The admitting paediatrician agrees to a full review of the past medical history and will consult with the trust's named professionals for safeguarding children.

Practice point

In his review of the circumstances of the death of Victoria Climbié, Laming (2003) coined the term 'respectful uncertainty' to describe an approach to ensure that professionals' assessments accurately determine the lived experience of the child. This seems to be especially important in FII where perpetrators normally enjoy good relationships with health professionals.

Fabricated or induced illness

FII is a recognized form of child physical abuse (HM Government 2010) and, as such, the focus of the care and treatment should always be on the safety and well-being of the child or young person. It is important that all health professionals are both knowledgeable about and alert to the risk of FII, while recognizing that it is best understood as occurring as a possibility within a spectrum of presentations of sick children. In some cases FII can cause tensions within and between health care teams who may be divided as to the possibility that parents or carers, who appear devoted and concerned, could deliberately harm their child. The need for support, supervision and debrief is important.

FII is a term that is used to describe either the fabrication of illness or disability in a well child, or exaggerating the severity of a known condition in a child (i.e. fabricating). It also refers to deliberately inducing symptoms (e.g. by poisoning or smothering), or promoting the sick role by withholding medication or treatment (i.e. inducing). Parents, particularly mothers, are the most common perpetrators, although others in a familial caring role may be implicated. In some cases there is collusion between parents. Perpetrators of this type of abuse are typically described as being knowledgeable and believable in their portrayal of the child's condition.

Practice point

Midwives need to be alert to the possibility of women inducing miscarriage or preterm birth. Women may also falsify their past obstetric histories (RCPCH 2009).

FII is a relatively rare condition (RCPCH 2009), but it is important in that it can cause children to undergo unnecessary, and often unpleasant, investigations and treatment, including surgery. FII can also lead to significant physical, behavioural and psychological problems for children, including confusion and anxiety about their health and adoption of a 'sick role'. Children and young people of all ages can be affected, although there is a preponderance of younger children and infants. There may be frequent absences from school and a lack of opportunity to take part in normal childhood activities.

In severe cases FII can lead to permanent disability or death. Importantly, it can take an average of nearly two years to identify children who may be suffering from this type of maltreatment, with an average age at diagnosis of 4 years, and boys and girls equally affected (NCCWCH 2009). There are recognized links with an increased risk of other forms of physical abuse and/or neglect both prior to, and subsequent to, diagnosis (RCPCH 2009).

According to the NCCWCH (2009) guidelines, the challenges to diagnosing (or confirming) FII include the reality that the symptoms that are described or induced are found in many common childhood illnesses. The guidelines also note that in some cases FII occurs *alongside* genuine conditions. There may be a pecuniary gain from exaggerating a degree of disability or chronic illness.

In an updated guide to the recognition and treatment of this challenging form of child maltreatment, the RCPCH (2009) proposes FII as part of a spectrum of presentations to child health professionals that include:

- parental anxiety;
- misperceptions and abnormal beliefs;
- parents'/carers' psychiatric illness;
- unrecognized genuine medical problem;
- presentations where a parent/carer has fabricated or induced their child's illness.

Each of the above possibilities will impact on the delivery of nursing care in the best interests of the child or young person. This may include meeting the child's and family's need for additional information, explanation, reassurance and support. It may also mean instigating the process of referral of the parent or carer to mental health services (via the GP). Where FII is suspected, referral to children's social care as a child protection concern is indicated. In some cases this can be lifesaving.

The following may occur in FII (adapted from RCPCH 2009: 7):

- deliberately inducing symptoms by administering medication or other substances;
- suffocation, inducing respiratory arrest;
- interfering with treatments by overdosing or by withholding medication;
- tampering with infusion lines or other medical devices;
- adding blood (e.g. menstrual) or other substances to specimens;
- claiming the child has physical symptoms such as fits, vomiting or diarrhoea, pain or psychological disorders (these are not witnessed by health care professionals);
- exaggeration of symptoms;
- making false entries on observation charts;
- seeking multiple opinions (including private consultations) and consulting with complementary medicine practitioners and alternative therapists;
- obtaining equipment for children which is not required (e.g. wheelchairs).

Case 3 continued

The team looking after Naimah makes a decision to review all previous records and to seek information from others who have had care of Naimah. The consultant paediatrician takes on a role as the responsible lead paediatrician to ensure that an accurate diagnosis is made. They will also ensure that the need for further tests and procedures is minimized to avoid the possibility of 'iatrogenic harm'[5] while the review is conducted (RCPCH 2009). Best practice dictates that in such cases the child and family are cared for by senior team members, with careful management of confidentiality, and support for the team. Sally, the ward sister, is thus allocated to manage Naimah's nursing care. In line with supplementary statutory guidance on the inter-agency management of suspected FII (HM Government 2008c), children's social care are contacted, and it is possible that they already hold information that may contribute to the review.

The lead paediatrician seeks Adriana's consent to request all previous health records, as a means to 'get to the root of the problem' (RCPCH 2009). Records in such cases are normally kept secure, to avoid tampering. Charting of symptoms, such as pain or diarrhoea, will need to be explicit and verified – i.e. date, time, reported by, witnessed by, child's view of events. The trust's named nurse, Mei (see Chapter 1) is asked to draw up a comprehensive health chronology that will detail all of Naimah's contacts with health professionals.

---

[5]The term iatrogenesis refers to unintentional harm or complications that arise from health care investigations or treatment.

In aiming to be focused on the safety and well-being of the child, it is important to ensure that their views and/or perspective are provided. A fully integrated chronology drawing on data from primary care, as well as secondary and tertiary care, will help to get a fuller picture of the possibility of FII. It is important to remember that most children will have genuine illness at some point during their childhood. An example of a template that can be used in this instance (and also for the purpose of serious case review, see Chapter 7) is given below.

Date	Time	Source of information/ professional	Description of event	Views of the child?	Reviewer's comments
12/08/10– 15/08/10		Hospital records Paediatrician	Re-referred by GP with reports from mother of continued loose stools and weight loss Jejeunal biopsy Abdominal X-Ray Bloods Urine screen - all NAD[6]	Seemed settled in hospital. Noted to be a little pale and quiet, reluctant to mix with other children	Mother resident and helping with care; stool chart incomplete?
6/07/10		Letter to GP from allergy specialist	Private appointment. Mother reports child has wheeze and rash. To return for skin tests	No history of wheeze given on previous attendance	
14/04/10	17:35	GP records	Mild sore throat: antibiotics prescribed as child reported to have been pyrexial and very unwell over the weekend		Verification of history?

---

[6]No abnormalities detected.

Producing a chronology is time-consuming, especially in cases where there have been a multiplicity of contacts with health care agencies. However, chronologies are incredibly valuable in helping to determine causes for concern about the possibility of FII. In my experience health data can be held in various locations and separate case notes, even within the same health care organization. The RCPCH (2009) guidance promotes the helpfulness of the use of one set of records for children and young people, including combining the nursing and medical records, and this practice was previously recommended by Laming (2003). The increasing use of electronic solutions for care recording and management will be beneficial, especially where care is accessed on a number of sites.

In considering the 'spectrum' of illness behaviour the following are possible findings and outcomes for Naimah:

- reassurance that there is no apparent clinical diagnosis; primary and community health professionals will arrange support to manage mother's anxiety;
- advice in terms of what may be considered to be 'normal' in relation to daily bowel habits and encouragement for Naimah to be independent in toileting;
- liaison with the GP, who will make a referral for mother to be seen by adult mental health services;
- discharge without a firm diagnosis and the possibility that a return of symptoms will lead to further interventions;
- discovery that the symptoms reported by mother cannot be verified by nursing records; mother also found to be falsifying charts;*
- when challenged on the basis of the chronology and review, mother admits that she has been administering large doses of laxatives to Naimah.*

*These findings will mean a child protection referral is made to children's social care.

Naimah: summary of concerns

Naimah has been readmitted to hospital with a history of reported ongoing gastrointestinal problems with no clear diagnosis. There are possibilities that Ariana has fabricated aspects of the reported illness, and nursing staff have been asked to draw together a detailed chronology and ensure that accurate records are kept.

Markers of good practice: the role of the named nurse safeguarding children

As a named nurse working in a specialist children's hospital it is likely that Mei will have been involved in previous cases of suspected FII.

Mei offers support and guidance to the team caring for Naimah, and helps to coordinate the retrieval of records from various health care agencies. She offers particular guidance and support to Sally.

Using a template, Mei pulls together a detailed chronology of all Naimah's contacts with health services. The completed chronology is extensive and runs to 36 pages.

Mei ensures that professionals involved in the case are aware of the supplementary guidance on management of FII (HM Government 2008c), and local LSCB procedures.

At the conclusion of the review, and after appropriate referrals have been made, Mei arranges for a debrief session for involved professionals.

Summary

This chapter has considered physical abuse, which can involve causing physical harm by deliberately injuring a child or by fabricating or inducing illness. The notions of statutory child protection referral and strategy discussions were also introduced. Although most physical abuse may be classified as being 'minor', in severe cases it can lead to permanent disability or death. Serious case reviews may highlight a pattern of progressive injuries over time, which, with the benefit of hindsight may suggest missed opportunities to recognize physical maltreatment. Nurses and midwives have a role in identifying children and young people who may be suffering from, or at risk of, physical abuse.

The three scenarios presented included non-accidental bruising in a young baby, deliberate burns in a toddler and a case involving a young girl that may prove to be fabricated or induced illness. They are not intended to be inclusive of all types of physical abuse but demonstrate the importance of nurses', midwives' and health visitors' roles and responsibilities, albeit they do not practise in isolation, but with other health care colleagues and those from other agencies. Apart from Mei, an experienced children's nurse and health visitor who now specializes in safeguarding children, the nurses in this chapter see a wider range of children, young people and their families. This, together with a child- and family-centred approach to assessment and openness to the possibility of child maltreatment, helps them to identify children and young people who may be at risk of, or suffering from, harm and to ensure their safety.

Key points

- Nurses and midwives who see children in the course of their practice should be familiar with child care and development and have a good understanding of indicators of possible child maltreatment.

- Health visitors and school nurses should be informed of all attendances at emergency departments/minor injuries units.
- A liaison health visitor/children's nurse can support information-sharing processes (two-way) between hospitals and community teams.
- Children attending for urgent care should have their child protection status checked.
- Children's social care is the lead agency for referral of child protection concerns; telephone referrals should be followed up in writing within 48 hours.
- Clear, contemporaneous records of events and actions should be kept.
- In cases of suspected FII a robust chronology detailing all contacts with health professionals should be drawn up.
- Support and advice on any aspect of safeguarding children can be obtained from named and designated professionals.

4 Emotional abuse

Learning outcomes

This chapter will help you to:

- Understand the features of emotional abuse as a form of child maltreatment.
- Identify indicators that may be associated with emotional abuse, including significant risk factors.
- Reflect on the potential safeguarding and child protection contribution of 'adult-centred' practitioners.
- Make a practical professional contribution to an initial child protection conference.
- Understand the role of the educational welfare officer.

Introduction

This chapter considers emotional abuse and the actions that nurses, midwives and health visitors can take to ensure that children and young people who may be suffering from emotional abuse are identified, and that appropriate help and support is provided. Emotional abuse takes many forms; what is important here is that it is likely to be contextual, rather than reflect an 'incident' (i.e. as compared to physical abuse). This means that nurses, midwives and health visitors who are providing ongoing care to a child, young person and their family are well placed to identify this form of maltreatment. As in the previous chapters, three practice-based scenarios will be discussed as a means of illustrating how nursing intervention can be critical in ensuring the safety and well-being of children and young people.

- Case 1: Poppy, aged 6 years, has been referred to child and adolescent mental health services (CAMHS) because of increasingly challenging behaviour. Her mother describes her as a child who is 'difficult to love'.
- Case 2: Tyra, aged 13 years, is the eldest child in a family of four children. Tyra's school attendance has been steadily declining and there are concerns that her parents' substance misuse difficulties have spiralled out of control.

- Case 3: Nilay, aged 9 years, suffers from severe cerebral palsy. He has recently been losing weight and has just had a procedure for a percutaneous endoscopic gastrostomy (PEG) feeding tube to provide enteral nutrition support.

As in the previous chapter, these examples are not intended to offer a fully comprehensive description of all the possible presentations of this form of child maltreatment. However, the cases do aim to provide insight into how emotional abuse may present in practice and the steps that nurses (including those whose role is primarily with the parent) should take to respond. Building on the knowledge gained in the previous chapter about the referral process to children's social care, and the subsequent strategy discussion to share information and context for concerns, this chapter introduces the initial child protection conference. The aim here is to help you to understand your role in contributing your nursing expertise to the conference and how decisions made at this multi-agency meeting plan for the future safety and protection of the child (or children in the family). Where the conference decision is to make a child subject to a statutory 'child protection plan' there will normally be specific actions within the plan for health professionals, especially those from universal services (i.e. midwives, health visitors, school nurses), albeit that this may include monitoring compliance with other health service provision, for example a child's attendance at a paediatric clinic or a parent's concordance with a substance misuse treatment programme. We begin by defining emotional abuse.

Emotional abuse

The *Working Together* (HM Government 2010) definition of emotional abuse offers a good understanding of the possible presentation of this form of maltreatment. Importantly, this definition also recognizes that emotional abuse, by its very nature, is a feature of all types of child maltreatment. As we noted in Chapter 3, the statutory definitions provided in the guidance are used to categorize the type of abuse for the purpose of child protection proceedings. However, the numbers of children and young people who are made the subject of a child protection plan under the category of emotional abuse are disproportionally small, at approximately a quarter of the total (DCSF 2009).
The *Working Together* definition of emotional abuse is as follows:

Emotional abuse is the persistent emotional maltreatment of a child such as to cause severe and persistent adverse effects on the child's emotional development. It may involve conveying to the child that they are worthless or unloved, inadequate, or valued only insofar as they meet the needs of another person. It may include not giving the child opportunities to express their views, deliberately silencing them or 'making fun' of what they say or how they communicate. It may feature age or developmentally inappropriate expectations being imposed upon children. These may include interactions that are beyond the child's developmental capability, as well as overprotection and limitation of exploration and learning, or preventing the child participating in normal social interaction. It may involve seeing or hearing the ill-treatment of another. It may involve bullying (including cyberbullying), causing children frequently to feel frightened or in danger, or the exploitation or corruption of children. Some level of emotional abuse is involved in all types of maltreatment of a child, though it may occur alone.

(HM Government 2010: 38)

The above definition is quite detailed and a simpler and helpful way to define and understand emotional maltreatment is the suggestion that it refers to 'a relationship rather than an event' (RCPCH 2006: 38). Nurses and midwives are likely to see children and young people at risk of, or suffering from, emotional maltreatment in the course of their work. This is because the risk factors for emotional abuse, outlined below, feature in families who are likely to be accessing health care in a variety of settings (adapted from RCPCH 2006). The risk factors are that:

- the child is the wrong sex;
- the child is unwanted;
- the child has a chronic illness or disability;
- the parents are experiencing relationship difficulties or domestic abuse;
- the parents themselves are vulnerable, including substance users or those with mental health difficulties.

Practice question

How can your assessment of child and family health needs help to identify the issues outlined above?

Parenting and emotional abuse

Identifying emotional abuse can be difficult, and it is widely believed that those cases that are identified as such by agencies represent only the 'tip of the iceberg'. One of the challenges is that this form of abuse is almost exclusively perpetrated by parents (or those in a parenting role) and that there is a very broad range of approaches to parenting and child care behaviour that may be seen in the course of practice. While there is clearly a debate to be held as to what constitutes 'good enough parenting' (being a perfect parent is likely to be beyond the reach of mere mortals!), it is interesting to note that the literature seems to more readily outline characteristics of *poor* parenting, rather than *good* parenting. In addition, there appears to be little in the way of concrete advice for practitioners on where the line may be drawn between the two.

In one article that seeks to provide a critique of the social, economic and political context of parenting, the authors list three times as many characteristics of poor parenting, as compared to good parenting (Taylor *et al.* 2000).

Table 4.1 Parenting characteristics

Characteristics of good parenting	Characteristics of poor parenting
✓ Teaching by example	• Exposure to deviant models
✓ Providing a secure environment	• Inability to provide continuity of care
✓ The mother's presence	• Poor supervision
✓ Attachment and bonding	• Lack of bonding and attachment
✓ Maturity	• Youth of the mother
✓ Unconditional affection	• Conditional affection
✓ Flexible control	• Cruel control
✓ Child-centredness	• Rejection
✓ Positive affectivity	• Negative affectivity
	• Unpredictability
	• Provocation
	• Impairment of health or development
	• Harmful or cruel discipline
	• Distance
	• Hostility
	• Intrusion
	• Poor mothering
	• Ignorance
	• Fecklessness
	• Lack of empathy for child
	• Unrealistic expectations
	• Laxity and inconsistency
	• Aggression
	• Low warmth
	• High criticism
	• Neglect
	• Abandonment

Source: adapted from Taylor et al. (2000: 114)

These characteristics, which might usefully inform midwifery and nursing assessment, are listed in Table 4.1.

Taylor et al. (2000) argue that achieving 'good enough parenting' is strongly influenced by the availability of resources and support. The authors express concern that while the socioeconomic determinants of the ability to parent well are evident, they are not always accounted for, and that the links between poverty and adverse outcomes in childhood need to be more widely appreciated and acted upon. Nurses, midwives and health visitors can be proactive in addressing inequalities in health through targeting services at those with the greatest need (i.e. ensuring needs-led, not demand-led, services). Taylor et al. also comment that the focus in the literature on parenting rests almost exclusively on 'mothering'; and this is clearly evident in their list of characteristics above. Parenting is a shared responsibility and the father's role (as we noted in Chapter 1) needs to be both recognized and promoted.

Cultural perspectives

A further dimension in ensuring informed assessment and decision-making in safeguarding and child protection is an appreciation of the cultural aspects of family life. Polnay *et al.* (2007) usefully explore ethnicity and cultural perspectives in child maltreatment and suggest that ethnic minority families are more likely to suffer from socioeconomic deprivation as well as being marginalized within society (they describe this as a 'double jeopardy'). The authors also suggest that there are a wide range of child care practices within multi-cultural Britain and argue for greater thought to be given to the assessment and care of ethnic minority families to avoid different standards of care being delivered to children and young people across the spectrum.

Race and ethnicity

The issue of race and ethnicity was brought into focus in the case of Victoria Climbié. Victoria, who was born in the Ivory Coast, came to the UK via France, in the care of her great-aunt. She subsequently suffered enduring and horrendous maltreatment, perpetrated by the great-aunt and the great-aunt's partner. Victoria died, aged 8 years, on 25 February 2000. Notably, Victoria was black African, and some of the front-line workers in the case were also of black heritage. The inquiry into the case noted that:

> Assumption based on race can be just as corrosive as blatant racism. Fear of being accused of racism can stop people acting when otherwise they would. Assumptions that people of the same colour, but from different backgrounds, behave in similar ways can distort judgements.
>
> (Laming 2003: 12)

On a practical basis nurses, midwives and health visitors may also need to consider access to professional interpreters to ensure that care is planned and delivered in an appropriate and timely manner. In general it is poor practice to use family members, especially children and young people, to act as interpreters in health and social care settings.

Prevention of emotional abuse

Nurses, midwives and health visitors may well have opportunities in the course of their practice to intervene to prevent emotional abuse. It is thus important to be able to recognize behaviours that may be indicative of a risk of this form of abuse. Barlow and Schrader-Macmillan (2009) describe a range of possible presentations, including:

- the emotional unavailability of parents;
- the parents attributing negative intentions, beliefs or attitudes towards the child;

- developmentally inappropriate interactions;
- the parents' lack of recognition of their roles and responsibilities;
- a failure to promote the child's social adaptation.

The authors also note that positive parenting programmes such as Triple P (see Chapter 1) and targeted home visiting programmes, such as the Family Nurse Partnership (FNP) programme (see Chapter 2) may help to prevent emotional abuse because of the emphasis that these programmes place on addressing emotionally abusive parenting (anger and misattributions). They also note the benefit of joined-up working between child and adult services. This means that it is vital that practitioners understand and enact the principles of information-sharing outlined in Chapter 1 and create systems of care delivery that are truly child- and family-centred.

The effects of emotional abuse are widely reported to include attachment and behavioural difficulties in childhood and poor cognitive and social functioning, mental health difficulties, self-harm and suicide in adulthood. Emotional abuse may thus precipitate difficulties in childhood that may be seen to be essentially 'behavioural' (e.g. aggression, challenging behaviour, withdrawal, low achievement), although these outcomes may also reflect other forms of child maltreatment (NCCWCH 2009). In identifying emotional abuse, it is always important to consider the daily lived experience of the child or young person and to focus on the meaning of parental difficulties and deficits on their well-being; this is why the RCPCH (2006) notion of a *relationship* rather than an *event* highlighted above is so important.

The following scenarios describe three different presentations of childhood emotional abuse. Links are made to the evidence base for practice and to statutory guidance. In each case the actions of the nurse are described in terms of best practice.

Case 1: Poppy — a 6-year-old child who is 'difficult to love'

Poppy is the first child of Siobhan, who has recently given birth to twin boys with a new partner. Poppy's father, who left the family before her birth, was known to be the perpetrator of serious domestic violence, and the pregnancy was unplanned. From the outset, Siobhan found Poppy to be a difficult child; she was a colicky baby, who was difficult to settle and did not sleep through the night until she was 11 months of age. Her mother continues to describe her as a 'fussy eater'. At the time of Poppy's birth Siobhan was living in somewhat sub-standard accommodation and in receipt of benefits. She was just 19 years of age and had left her childhood home and the town in which she grew up two years previously, following a serious disagreement with her mother. Although Siobhan has made some friends in the apartment block where she now lives, it has taken a while to build up her supportive network, and this has been aggravated by a shortage of money and difficulties in accessing child care. With a new relationship and the subsequent birth of the twins, the situation for Siobhan and the family has improved somewhat, despite the fact that the birth of twins is a significant source of challenge in any family. Siobhan now has a caring partner who is in employment. This new partner has also been able to take on some parenting responsibility for Poppy, even though he agrees with Siobhan that Poppy's behaviour is rather unpredictable and challenging. Both parents clearly adore the boys.

Poppy's health records show that there was repeated contact with universal and specialist services in her first few years of life, with referrals made to a primary mental health worker, a family centre and Home-Start.[1] There were also reports of frequent temper tantrums and destructive behaviour which had been observed by a number of professionals who visited, including the health visitor. Those who had contact with Poppy in the pre-school years were sympathetic to the difficulties her mother faced; but as well as witnessing the negative behaviour, they were also often greeted with smiles and demands for a cuddle. Although professionals felt uncomfortable about admitting that there was little more that could be offered, they could not help but agree that Poppy was, in her mother's words, 'a devil of a child'.

In order to provide some respite to the difficulties that she presented to her mother, Poppy was able to access a funded placement at nursery just before her third birthday. However, her attendance was poor and she required considerable support in gaining the confidence to play with the other children. On a more positive note, the nursery staff reported that Poppy was a child who sought to please, however they added that she was rather quiet and attributed this to a delay in her speech development. A referral for Poppy to be seen by a speech and language therapist had been made by the health visitor, but after she was not taken to two appointments her name was removed from the waiting list.

Practice point

Over-friendliness with strangers and attention-seeking behaviour in young children may indicate a problematic attachment. An insecure attachment can be a feature of emotional abuse and other forms of child maltreatment (NCCWCH 2009).

Poppy is now at primary school and is in Year 1. Her teachers assess that she is a bright child, who is not reaching her potential. She is often unhappy and appears to have difficulties in making friends, in part because she has a tendency to be spiteful. Following a discussion at a parent–teacher evening, where concerns about Poppy's behaviour were once again raised, Siobhan takes Poppy to the GP and a referral is made to CAMHS. Joe, who is a mental health nurse and has specialized in CAMHS, sees Poppy and her mother at a tier-two clinic (see below for an explanation of the CAMHS four-tier strategic framework). A provisional diagnosis of oppositional defiant disorder is made.

---

[1] See www.home-start.org.uk/homepage.

CAMHS four-tier strategic framework

The CAMHS four-tier strategic framework is a widely accepted conceptual framework for the commissioning, planning and delivery of services to children and young people who are experiencing mental health difficulties.

Tier one services are delivered by practitioners who are not mental health specialists, such as health visitors, school nurses and GPs. They will promote good mental health, offer general advice and treatment for less severe problems and refer to more specialist services where necessary. An example would be intervention offered in a case of mild anxiety that is beginning to affect everyday functioning and well-being.

Tier two services are offered by CAMHS specialists, such as primary mental health workers, psychologists and counsellors working in community and primary care settings. They will offer consultation to families and other practitioners, outreach to identify severe or complex needs and training to non-specialist practitioners working at tier one. An example would be intervention in conduct disorders.

Tier three services are usually provided by a multi-disciplinary team working in a community mental health clinic or child psychiatry outpatient department. The team will provide more specialized care for children, young people and their families with more severe, complex or persistent disorders such as obsessive-compulsive rituals.

Tier four comprises highly specialist, often regionally-based services for children and young people with the most serious mental health difficulties. Care may be provided by outpatient teams or within inpatient facilities. These may include forensic adolescent units, eating disorder units, specialist neuro-psychiatric units and intensive care. An example of tier-four care would be for a young person at high risk of serious self-harm.

Note: following pressure from the UK's Children's Commissioners, all children and young people under the age of 18 years with mental health problems that require an inpatient stay should be cared for within CAMHS facilities (Office of the Children's Commissioner/Young Minds 2007).

Oppositional defiant disorder

Oppositional defiant disorder (ODD) is a term used to describe disobedient, hostile and defiant behaviour that goes beyond that which may be considered 'normal' in childhood. While it can be linked to those who have a difficult temperament, attention deficit disorder (ADD) or learning difficulties, it can also present as a result of bullying and abuse (Royal College of Psychiatrists 2004). Treatment can take a variety of forms, including parenting programmes, individual or family psychotherapy and cognitive behavioural therapy (CBT).

In some cases, particularly as a first line of provision, input from a primary mental health worker can be helpful.

Case 1 continued

Working very closely with Siobhan, Poppy and her stepfather, Joe, the CAMHS practitioner, devises a programme of tailored therapy that includes a focus on positive parenting techniques. These will not only be helpful to Poppy, but also serve as a useful adjunct to ensure that the twins are parented in a way that will promote good mental health for the future. Joe liaises with the family health visitor, GP and the school. His review of the records reflects his concerns that Poppy was somewhat of a scapegoat for her mother's difficulties surrounding the violent and destructive relationship with Poppy's father. He is also concerned that previous professionals have demonstrated sympathy and support for Siobhan with her housing and financial problems and her 'difficult child' and failed to respond to the fact that this mother had frequently sought to express a real difficulty in loving a child who resulted from a brutal relationship with the father. Joe judges there to be early evidence of an emotionally abusive relationship between parent and child, whereby Siobhan has been unable to develop a responsive and protective relationship with her daughter. Furthermore, it is concerning that this mother has expressed negativity in the presence of professionals who floundered in their ability to offer a helpful response. In summary, Joe feels that there is past evidence of emotional abuse and a failure by professionals to consider the best interests of the child. He discusses these concerns with his supervisor.

Markers of good practice: the role of the health care team

The case of Poppy demonstrates what can happen when professionals are drawn to the (very real) problems of parents and lose sight of the best interests of the child.

Poppy was born in very difficult circumstances and by her own admission Siobhan felt that she was a 'difficult child to love'. Early input from the health visitor and others should have ensured that additional support and advice was aimed at developing mother–child attachment through a more positive and child-centred approach.

Joe appears to be the first professional who has focused on the meaning of the parental difficulties for the child and the impact of an emotionally abusive relationship on the development of ODD. More attention should have been given to the fact that the nursery did not witness the degree of challenging behaviour that was reported to be happening at home, as well as the reported 'over-friendliness' with strangers.

Joe completes clear, contemporaneous records of the events and his actions (NMC 2009b). He also follows local clinical supervision policy in recording the outcomes and actions from his deliberations with his supervisor.

There will be a need to review the situation and consider whether any current concerns, or failure to respond to treatment, should lead to a referral to children's social care.

Case 2: Tyra — a 'little mother' to her siblings

Tyra is 13 years old and in Year 9 at school. She has three younger siblings, the youngest of which is 22 months old. Lately Tyra has been either missing school, or arriving late looking somewhat tired and distracted. Her school work is suffering. School teaching staff are concerned that she will slip further behind with her studies at a time when she should be focusing her thoughts on her GCSE choices for the following year. They discuss their concerns that all is not well at home with the school nurse and the education welfare officer.

A decision is made that, in the first instance, Tyra should be persuaded to see the school nurse at the lunchtime drop-in session; if there is little visible improvement in attendance and demeanour then the educational welfare officer will pick up the case. When the school nurse meets Tyra, she is noticeably pale and quiet. Eventually it transpires that she has been providing care for her younger siblings, including managing shopping on a very limited budget, preparing meals and feeding and bathing the toddler. She has also been taking the middle two children to their primary school most days. The school is located about half a mile from her secondary school. At the weekends Tyra has been cleaning and washing clothes. She has not been seeing her friends lately. Tyra's overriding concerns are for her parents, Tracy and Dave, who have been staying in bed and are sometimes angry or difficult to arouse. Despite trying to keep on top of things, Tyra is very ashamed of the state of the house and is worried about the increasingly clingy behaviour of her toddler brother. Tyra's parents are known to have problems with alcohol, and are also thought to have used heroin and benzodiazepines in the past. The local substance misuse service has previously been involved with the family and the GP will re-refer. Tyra is extremely cautious about sharing her story, expressing a wish for the family to stay together and for things to be 'like they used to be'. Tyra is effectively a 'child carer' whose needs for a safe and secure childhood in which she can achieve her full potential are not being met. All of the children are at risk of suffering from neglect and emotional abuse. After seeking support from her manager, and discussing her concerns for the children's well-being at a home visit to the parents, the school nurse makes a child protection referral to children's social care services.

Parental substance misuse

According to figures highlighted in guidance for schools on supporting pupils of parents who have substance misuse difficulties, there are currently thought to be as many as 335,000 children in the UK living with parental drug dependency and more than a million living with problematic parental alcohol use (The Princess Royal Trust for Carers/The Children's Society 2010). As the guidance notes, these children and young people are often engaged in providing physical care and emotional support to their parents, as well as coping with household chores and the care of siblings. It adds that these child carers can find it very difficult to seek help from agencies because they are concerned about the stigma of parental substance misuse, a feeling of betrayal of their parents and the impact of any likely intervention on their family life. The guidance also acknowledges the dangers and risks faced by children and young people within the context of parental substance misuse (e.g. from drug paraphernalia, others visiting the household, or the increased likelihood of becoming users themselves) and calls for school nurses to be available to support affected pupils' health and well-being and to undertake home visits to their families. The links to safeguarding and child protection are acknowledged.

Although a great deal has been achieved in terms of better recognition and response to the issues raised by problematic parental substance misuse in recent years, it is still seen as an area where improvements can be made. Much activity in this field follows the report on *Hidden Harm* published in 2003 following an inquiry by the Advisory Council on the Misuse of Drugs (ACMD). The report contains a number of recommendations, some of which are specifically aimed at early years, schools and health services, including those dealing specifically with drug and alcohol problems. However, the overarching messages from the work include the recognition of the serious risk of harm to children of all ages (i.e. from conception to adulthood) and the benefits to children of successful treatment of the parental substance misuse problems. *Hidden Harm* recognizes that by working together services can take many practical steps to protect and improve the health and well-being of affected children and young people. Substance misuse services are thus asked to forge links with and between maternity, child health and children's social care services, and to work in a coordinated and integrated way to benefit the children of problematic substance misusing parents.

Two of the *Hidden Harm* recommendations are aimed specifically at substance misuse services: 'Drug and alcohol agencies should recognise that they have a responsibility towards the dependent children of their clients and aim to provide accessible and effective support for parents and their children, either directly or through good links with other relevant services' and 'The training of staff in drug and alcohol agencies should include a specific focus on learning how to assess and meet the needs of clients as parents and their children' (ACMD 2003: 17).

The use of the *Framework for the Assessment of Children in Need and their Families* (DH 2000) is promoted by the ACMD which, whilst recognizing that this is essentially a tool that is used by social workers, suggests that it has a place for use by professionals from health and educational agencies with families where there is problematic parental substance misuse. In addition to the domains and headings highlighted in the assessment triangle (i.e. those listed under 'child's developmental factors', 'family and environmental' and 'parenting capacity') it is suggested that the following supplementary headings are considered (ACMD 2003: 80):

- parental drug use;
- accommodation and the home environment;
- provision of basic needs;
- procurement of drugs;
- health risks;
- family and social supports;
- parents' perception of the situation.

Consideration of the above factors will help professionals to address the impact of parental substance misuse on the ability to parent. The suggestions also recognize that these families are often struggling with other related issues such as poor physical and mental health, domestic abuse, financial difficulties, social isolation and poor housing.

While this section has sought to promote the importance of substance misuse services' assessment of the needs of the children and young people of parental substance misusers, and their engagement with child and family services, it is important to note that there may have been a tradition of the failure of child and family services (i.e. midwifery, health visiting and school nursing) to engage proactively and appropriately with substance misuse services. As Cleaver *et al.* (2008) note, relationships between services can be compromised by concerns about confidentiality and negative preconceptions of parents with problem drug or alcohol use. This needs to be tackled. Nurses, midwives and health visitors can be at the forefront of improving the health, well-being and functioning of the family through informed and non-judgemental care, considered information-sharing and joint working, and keeping the needs of the child and the quality of parenting in focus.

Case 2 continued

Fred, a mental health nurse by background, is a member of the multidisciplinary substance misuse community team which provides tier-three[2] services including stabilization, detoxification and counselling in cases of complex substance misuse and dependency. He has been allocated as the key worker for Dave and Tracy. Fred's care plan identifies the needs of the parents, Tyra and the other children and aims to do the following:

- stabilize, and then reduce, the parents' substance misuse, working towards detoxification and abstinence;

---

[2]Like CAMHS, substance misuse services are provided within a four-tier framework.

- liaise with the health visitor and school nurse to ensure that the children's health needs are met;
- support the parents to ensure that the elder three children are attending school.

In addition, Fred will liaise with children's social care. His role here is to provide support and advice to children's social care in planning to best meet the needs of the children. Because of the intense nature of his input, he may also be the first professional to recognize any deterioration in parenting or additional concerns about the well-being of the children. It is likely that social care will consider these children as being at risk of emotional abuse, and also of neglect. If a decision is made to proceed to child protection enquiries, then Fred will contribute to these together with other colleagues from health services. However, his contribution will not replace the input of core universal services. These responsibilities are nicely summed up in the *Hidden Harm* document as follows: 'In their efforts to help the children of clients, we believe that drug agencies should concentrate upon doing the basics well and liaising closely with other agencies rather than attempting too much themselves' (ACMD 2003: 83). This is sound advice and, if followed, could be instrumental in bringing about a step-change in tackling some of the traditions of poor intra- and inter-agency working and engagement that have been seen in practice and are highlighted in the literature.

The initial child protection conference

Many children who become subject to a child protection plan will have parents who misuse substances (Cleaver *et al.* 2008). In the case of Tyra and her siblings, continuing concerns from child health, substance misuse and educational services about the behaviours of the parents and the welfare of the children are such that a strategy discussion is held and a decision made to initiate 'Section 47' (i.e. child protection) enquiries.

As a key professional providing care to parents who are experiencing substance misuse problems, Fred engages with the statutory child protection processes (HM Government 2010), notably by providing information on the parents' treatment programmes, their concordance with the treatment and the functional impact of their addiction.

Enquiries under Section 47 of the Children Act 1989

Section 47 sets out the duties of the local authority (i.e. children's social care services) in making enquiries to decide whether compulsory intervention is needed to safeguard or promote the welfare of a child. It also places agencies, such as health services, under a duty to assist the local authority in carrying out such enquiries.

The local authority children's social care department has the lead responsibility for undertaking a 'core assessment' using the *Framework for the Assessment of Children in Need and their Families* (DH 2000) that will help to collect and organize the information gathered in the course of their enquiries. This will build on the initial assessment that would have been undertaken at the point at which concerns about the well-being of the children were raised. Obtaining children and young people's views and wishes is crucial to the process and it is important that they have an opportunity to be seen both with, and without, their parents or carers. However, working constructively with parents is very important because 'in the great majority of cases, children remain with their families following Section 47 enquiries, even where concerns about abuse or neglect are substantiated' (HM Government 2010: 158).

Initial child protection conferences (also known as ICPCs) are normally held within 15 working days of a strategy discussion's decision to initiate Section 47 enquiries. This is an opportunity to bring together family members, the child (where appropriate) and the professionals who are most involved with the child and family. The purpose of an ICPC is to:

- bring together and analyse the information that has been obtained in relation to the child's health and developmental needs and the parents' ability to meet these needs within the context of the family and environment;
- make a judgement on the harm suffered by the child and the likelihood of the child suffering significant harm in the future; and
- decide what future action will be needed to safeguard and promote the welfare of the child in the future, including whether the child should be made the subject of a child protection plan.

Initial child protection conferences can be very large gatherings, and this carries with it the risk that the children and families who are the subject of the conference may feel intimidated. An initial child protection conference will typically involve the following:

- the child, if they are of an appropriate age/understanding;
- family members (parents and sometimes extended family such as grandparents);
- advocates for the child or family;
- an independent reviewing officer (IRO) who will chair the conference;
- children's social care staff, including the lead social worker who has undertaken the assessment;
- professionals involved with the children (e.g. midwife, health visitor or school nurse, CAMHS practitioner, GP, early years or teaching staff, paediatrician);
- professionals involved with the parents (e.g. mental health or substance misuse practitioners, GP);
- those involved in the investigations (e.g. the police);
- local authority legal services (child care).

The role of the IRO

Formal child protection conferences are highly likely to be stressful for children, young people and their families due to the nature of the concerns and the professional scrutiny of parenting and family life. There is frequently sociocultural diversity between professionals and the family. The IRO ensures that diversity is considered, that families are put at ease and that all those present understand the purpose of the conference and how it will be conducted (see HM Government 2010: 164–5 for more details).

The nursing contribution

Nurses, midwives and health visitors who are invited to attend an initial child protection conference will be expected to bring details of their involvement with the child and family to the conference. This will be in the form of written reports that will include details of involvement with the family, and a chronology of significant events. These should be prepared to reflect the *Framework for Assessment* domains and include practitioners' knowledge of the child's developmental needs and the capacity of the parents to meet those needs within their family and environmental context (DH 2000). A good quality report will include an analysis that reflects both strengths and difficulties within the domains. Resilience and protective factors should be considered in balance with the level of vulnerability and risk. In providing information to an initial child protection conference it is important to be able to distinguish between fact, observation, allegation and opinion. Information may be provided from another source, but this should be made clear.

A report from a health visitor, for example, may include:

- name, qualifications and employer, how long employed in current post and how long family have been known to the practitioner;
- demographic details of the family including who is in the household and names and relationships of significant others;
- brief chronology of health visiting contacts with the family (e.g. core universal programme or targeted programme, dates of contacts, assessment of parental engagement and compliance);
- details of child's (or children's) health and developmental needs, including their presentation and demeanour, any specific health problems and unmet needs (physical, social and emotional);
- an assessment of the parental capacity to meet the health and developmental needs of the child (or children), including an assessment of capacity to change;
- details of the wider family and environment, including housing and social integration;

- an analysis of the future safety, health and developmental needs of the child or children, and how these may be met.

Child protection case conference reports should be shared with the family in advance of the conference. It is also usual practice for the report to be shared with, or signed off by, a manager prior to the conference.

The form and function of the initial child protection conference

As noted above, the initial child protection conference can be a large gathering of family members and professionals. Although the length of time a conference takes will be dependent on the complexity of the case, as well as the number of children in the family, proceedings normally take about two hours. Under the direction of the IRO, and following a round of introductions, those attending an initial child protection conference will begin by sharing their reports (with the social worker normally giving their report and outlining the concerns at the outset). The information gathered will build and present a rich tapestry of the daily lived experiences of the child or young person and help to inform the actions and decisions for the conference. Parents (and where age-appropriate the child or young person) will be able to respond to concerns raised and the IRO will ensure that opportunities are made available to clarify any points of uncertainty or challenge.

After hearing from the family and professionals, the IRO will seek to sum up the child protection concerns that have been expressed and invite agency representatives to express an opinion as to whether or not there is a need for a statutory child protection plan (see Chapter 5). This will then be enacted on the basis of a majority decision that the child has suffered, or is likely to suffer, significant harm, and is, or remains, at risk of suffering significant harm in the future. The IRO will also direct the conference in determining which category of abuse or neglect will be recorded. Where there is more than one child in a family, a separate discussion will take place for each child.

Tyra and her siblings: subject to a child protection plan

In the case of Tyra and her siblings, concerns shared at the initial child protection conference were such that a decision was made that Tyra would be made subject to a child protection plan under the category of 'emotional abuse'. The IRO concluded the decision-making by reflecting the fact that there were 'age or developmentally inappropriate expectations being imposed upon [her]' (HM Government 2010: 38). In addition, Tyra's siblings were made subject to a plan because they were considered to be at risk of neglect. The health visitor, the school nurse and the substance misuse nurse will all have a part to play in the core group of professionals and family members that will develop and implement the plan. At the end of the initial child protection conference dates were set for a core group meeting and the first review child protection conference (see Chapter 6).

Markers of good practice: the role of the substance misuse nurse

Fred acknowledges that he has a role in the assessment of the needs of any children where there is parental substance misuse. He is particularly concerned to ensure that Tyra is able to attend school and take part in activities with her peer group – i.e. to ensure that there are no 'age or developmentally inappropriate expectations being imposed upon [her]' that are indicative of emotional abuse (HM Government 2010: 38).

Tyra is provided with preventative advice and support in relation to the increased potential for her to become a user. Ensuring that she achieves her potential at school and is able to maintain a friendship group are important factors in achieving self-esteem and resilience.

Fred completes a care plan that includes the steps to be taken to ensure the needs of the children are met and liaises with universal health services (GP, health visitor and school nurse). He seeks consent from Dave and Tracy to share information appropriately in line with information sharing guidelines (HM Government 2008b).

Fred monitors the well-being of the children from his perspective of the impact of parental substance misuse on the ability to provide good enough parenting and liaises with children's social care accordingly. He seeks advice from his safeguarding leads (named professionals) where necessary.

Fred attends the strategy discussion and the initial child protection conference, for which he produces a report. The report outlines his care plans for the family and the engagement of Dave and Tracy in their treatment regimes, and includes an analysis of strengths and difficulties. The report is shared with the family prior to the conference.

Fred completes clear, contemporaneous records of the events and his actions (NMC 2009b). He also follows local clinical supervision policy in recording the outcomes and actions from his deliberations with his supervisor.

Case 3: Nilay – a hidden child

Nilay is 9 years old and has cerebral palsy with associated spastic quadriplegia and communication difficulties. He is the third child of Asha and Taj, and was born overseas at 29 weeks' gestation following a difficult pregnancy. Nilay's disability means that he requires a high level of care to meet his basic needs; however, his parents have been reluctant to allow professionals into the home and have been largely managing the care themselves, with some additional help from extended family. Nilay has recently been unwell with a series of chest infections and is becoming increasingly frail. Following a routine paediatric review a decision was made for Nilay to have a percutaneous endoscopic gastrostomy (PEG) feeding tube to provide enteral nutrition support, with the anticipation that an increased intake of calories and protein would improve his physical well-being and help to prevent infection.

Vicky, a children's community nurse, calls to see Nilay and his family at home to support the management of his new feeding regime. On entering the home Vicky is greeted by Nilay's parents and elder sisters and taken to the living room where she was surprised to see little evidence of the equipment usually associated with children with similar needs. Nilay, it transpires, is in his room, being a ground floor annexe at the back of the main house. A grandmother sleeps in an adjacent room.

As this is her first visit to the family, Vicky undertakes a detailed holistic assessment to support her care planning. She considers the need for an interpreter for supporting her communication with Nilay and his parents, but finds that Taj is able to translate for his wife, where needed. Vicky discovers that while Nilay appears to be reasonably well cared for physically, he is not currently receiving any formal education. His parents report that they felt that there was no suitable provision, and lay claim to providing some input themselves. Vicky's overriding concern is that Nilay is somewhat hidden from others. She discusses her unease with her manager, as she is worried that Nilay's isolation and apparent lack of interaction with other children, including somewhat limited contact with his siblings, may be affecting his opportunities to reach his potential, albeit that this is limited by his special needs. This state of affairs has been recognized in a study undertaken by Robert and Harris (2002) who found that immigrants and asylum-seeking families had a greater fear of being seen as 'doubly' different where family members were disabled.

Multiple challenges

The challenges for professionals in this case are numerous. As we discuss in the following chapter, children with a learning or physical disability are at greater risk of child maltreatment, but less likely to have concerns about possible harm raised (Murray and Osborne 2009). Nilay's parents and family appear devoted, however, as the statutory definition notes: 'overprotection and limitation of exploration and learning, or preventing the child participating in normal social interaction' is indicative of emotional abuse (HM Government 2010: 38).

In addition to the challenges provided by this complex case, it is my experience that children's community nurses do not necessarily have the same traditions of safeguarding and child protection skills and awareness as, for example, health visitors and school nurses. This may be due in part to a lack of appropriate learning opportunities and access to named professionals and others for specialist supervision. However, anecdotally, I have witnessed a tendency for these practitioners to develop very close relationships with parents and carers, who themselves are often struggling with the physical, emotional and financial burdens of caring for a child with complex needs. This state of affairs can lead to a failure by children's community nurses to consider the daily lived experience of the child. Thus, Vicky is likely to need a high degree of support and access to good 'child protection' oriented supervision to allow her to advocate for Nilay and to ensure that he is given the maximum opportunity to develop his potential. Importantly, her skills in child-centred assessment have enabled her to identify that his needs are currently not being met.

Nilay: next steps

With the support of her manager and the named nurse safeguarding children, Vicky arranges a professional network meeting to share her concerns about Nilay's isolation and educational needs. Those in the children's disability team attend. The team were already aware of the fact that Nilay had become physically frail. However, it transpired that, with the exception of a paediatric occupational therapist who has undertaken home visits to assist and advise on home adaptations, Nilay has generally been seen in a community clinic or hospital setting. Therefore the concerns about his apparent seclusion and the impact that this may have on his emotional well-being had not been identified previously. In addition, there is also a possibility that the cultural diversity of the family (including language differences) has proved to be a barrier.

The *Framework for the Assessment of Children in Need and their Families* (DH 2000) includes a useful section on the child's developmental needs in relation to education. Here it is noted that education provides opportunities:

- for play and interaction with other children;
- to access books;
- to acquire a range of skills and interests;
- to experience success and achievement.

Nilay is missing out on these opportunities. The social worker for children with disabilities was asked to liaise with child protection colleagues in social care to consider a core assessment of Nilay's health and developmental needs and to identify the best way forward in working with his family to ensure that these are met.

Markers of good practice: the role of the children's community nurse

In her provision of care Vicky demonstrates 'sensitivity to differing family patterns and lifestyles and an understanding that child-rearing patterns can vary across different racial, ethnic and cultural groups' (HM Government 2010: 286), yet maintains a child-centred approach to recognize concerns.

Vicky seeks supervision from her manager and initiates a professional network meeting to share her concerns and to consider next actions.

Vicky completes clear, contemporaneous records of the events and her actions (NMC 2009b).

Summary

This chapter has considered emotional abuse in childhood. As noted at the outset, emotional abuse is present in all forms of child maltreatment, but may occur on its own. The statutory definition of emotional abuse describes a range of situations of concern, but it may be best summarized as 'a relationship rather than an event'. Thus this form of abuse will most typically involve difficulties in the parent–child relationship. The three scenarios outlined in this chapter describe emotional abuse in the context of an unloved child who develops ODD, an adolescent who takes responsibility for the care of her parents and siblings and a disabled child whose developmental needs are compromised by a lack of opportunity for education and social interaction with his peers. The nursing staff involved in these fictitious cases included a CAMHS practitioner, a substance misuse nurse and a community children's nurse. The unifying feature in terms of taking action to safeguard and promote the welfare of these children was the ability of these professionals to consider the 'daily lived experience' of the child.

Key points

- Nurses and midwives who see children in the course of their practice should be familiar with child care and development and have a sound understanding of indicators of possible child maltreatment.
- An understanding of the features of good parenting is helpful in the prevention, early identification and response to emotional abuse.
- Assessments of children in need consider the child's developmental factors, family and environmental factors and parenting capacity.
- Sensitivity to race, culture and ethnicity is important, however, child abuse cannot be condoned for religious or cultural reasons.
- Child protection conferences should consider strengths and protective factors, as well as risks.

5 Sexual abuse

Learning outcomes

This chapter will help you to:

- Understand the features of sexual abuse as a form of child maltreatment.
- Be able to identify indicators and behaviours that may be associated with sexual abuse in the course of your practice.
- Recognize that sexual exploitation is a form of child abuse.
- Develop your understanding of the increased risk of child maltreatment for children and young people with disabilities.
- Make a professional contribution to a child protection plan.
- Know how to respond to a disclosure of behaviour that is indicative of child sexual abuse.

Introduction

This chapter considers child sexual abuse and begins by outlining the defining attributes of this form of maltreatment and the possible presenting indicators. Following the format of the previous chapters, three fictitious scenarios, which are based on the reality of practice in cases of sexual abuse, are presented. As before, these practical examples cannot be fully inclusive of the range of behaviours and features of this form of abuse, but are intended to trigger the development of knowledge and understanding that will help nurses and midwives to be confident and competent in recognizing and responding to child maltreatment.

- Case 1: Marnie, aged 14 years, is attending a young persons' contraception and sexual health clinic with a friend. She is requesting a pregnancy test.
- Case 2: Jodie, a 10-year-old with progressive learning disabilities, has begun attending a respite care facility provided by the local children's hospice. She and her family are supported by Marcus, a registered nurse (learning disability), who provides an outreach service from the hospice.
- Case 3: Stewart, who is an adult mental health service client, discloses that he has been accessing child pornography on the internet.

Building on the knowledge and understanding that you have gained about the pathway for child protection referral, the strategy discussion, the Children Act 1989 Section 47 (child protection enquiries), and the initial child protection conference, this chapter introduces the child protection plan. The plan, which follows the initial child protection conference consensus decision that a child or young person may be at continuing risk of significant harm, informs the process by which agencies work together with children, young people and their families to ensure their future safety and protection. Nurses and midwives from both universal and specialist services may have a key role in leading, or supporting, actions that are outlined in the plan. We begin by defining sexual abuse.

Sexual abuse

The *Working Together* (HM Government 2010: 38) definition of sexual abuse is as follows:

> Sexual abuse involves forcing or enticing a child or young person to take part in sexual activities, not necessarily involving a high level of violence, whether or not the child is aware of what is happening. The activities may involve physical contact, including assault by penetration (for example, rape or oral sex) or non-penetrative acts such as masturbation, kissing, rubbing and touching outside of clothing. They may also include non-contact activities, such as involving children looking at, or in the production of, sexual images, watching sexual activities, encouraging children to behave in sexually inappropriate ways, or grooming a child in preparation for abuse (including via the internet). Sexual abuse is not solely perpetrated by adult males. Women can also commit acts of sexual abuse, as can other children.

Polnay *et al.* (2007) note that the notion of child sexual abuse being part of the spectrum of mainstream child maltreatment occurred some 20 years after child physical abuse was first highlighted to health professionals. This was, they add, in spite of the fact that sexual abuse had been raised as a possible form of harm in childhood many years previously by pioneers such as Freud. Society's acceptance of the existence of this form of maltreatment has seemingly lagged behind that of professionals, although arguably it remains a taboo subject across the board. This means that sufferers may experience difficulty in telling their story and ultimately receiving care and protection. Such difficulties can be compounded by the fact that the sexually abused child may be unaware that what they are experiencing is abusive, in part because they may have been 'groomed' by their perpetrator.

Quotes from adult survivors of child sexual abuse

'Why do I feel so bad, like it was my fault? I didn't know what was happening to me at the time. I didn't even know what sex was . . .'
'He used to say to me that this was our secret and I should never tell anyone, especially mum and dad (I didn't).'
'When I was thirteen, I suddenly connected what he was doing to me with playground dirty jokes . . .'
'If I had had someone to talk to that I could trust, I may have opened up but my problem was that I was full of fear and could not bring myself to talk to someone . . .'

(National Commission of Inquiry into the Prevention of
Child Abuse 1996: 170–2)

The number of children and young people who are made subject to a child protection plan because they are at risk of, or suffering from, sexual abuse appears to be declining at a time when overall numbers of children subject to a plan are increasing, with approximately 6 per cent of plans being made within this category of abuse.[1] However, such figures do not bear witness to the reported prevalence of this form of maltreatment. The study by Cawson *et al.* (2000), highlighted in previous chapters, is particularly helpful in determining the statistics for child sexual abuse. This is because it draws on the experiences of young adults from across the population, rather than simply those who come to the attention of statutory child protection agencies. Mirroring the definition of sexual abuse outlined above, Cawson *et al.* found that 11 per cent of boys and 21 per cent of girls reported experiencing some form of child sexual abuse during the course of their childhood. The abuse was reported to occur most often within the context of family or those known to the young people, and more rarely was perpetrated a stranger or someone they had just met. In relation to non-familial sexual abuse, the perpetrator was most likely to be a boyfriend or girlfriend, but fellow students and friends of parents or siblings were also mentioned. Sexual abuse by someone in a position of trust (e.g. teacher, religious leader or care/social worker) was said to be rare and occurred in less than 1 per cent of the reported cases.

Perpetrators and victims of child sexual abuse are drawn from across the social spectrum. However, certain groups are noted to be at greater risk of harm and these include disabled children (Murray and Osborne 2009), children in care and those whose parents are experiencing adult mental health or substance misuse problems (Nelson 2009). This finding has important implications for health professionals who will be providing care to such groups and therefore in a position to recognize and respond to children and young people at risk of sexual abuse, including being open to a disclosure. Nevertheless, it is

---

[1] See www.nspcc.org.uk/Inform/research/statistics (accessed 10 October 2010), which provides a five-year summary of child protection statistics for all four countries of the UK.

also important to be aware of the difficulties that children and young people have in disclosing sexual maltreatment. For example, Cawson *et al.*'s (2000) study found that the majority of children and young people who have experienced child sexual abuse (i.e. some three-quarters) do not tell anyone about it at the time. Although the study also reported that a proportion of victims do go on to disclose, a third of those who had reported being sexually abused as a child had not shared their experience at the time of their interview, reflecting in turn the stories of those giving evidence to the National Commission of Inquiry into the Prevention of Child Abuse (1996). Nelson (2009: 24) summarizes the reasons for non-disclosure of childhood sexual abuse in childhood and adulthood as 'deep shame, self-blame, fear of other children's rejection, fear of retaliation and the expectation (often realistic) of being disbelieved'.

These are fundamental issues for nurses and midwives. An acknowledgement of the existence and prevalence of child sexual abuse, and the difficulties that victims encounter in disclosing their experiences, are key factors in offering a helpful and therapeutic response.

Practice question

Nelson (2009) suggests that for a worried young person or adult to confide abuse within a health care setting professionals need to:

- be welcoming;
- create an atmosphere of respect;
- be receptive to the possibility of child sexual abuse;
- be sensitive; and
- offer open-minded, non-judgemental listening.

How can this be assured in your area of practice?

Indicators of child sexual abuse

Drawing on the evidence-based guidelines published by the RCPCH (2008), the NCCWCH guidelines (2009: 47) conclude that observable signs of child sexual abuse are 'relatively uncommon'. The guidelines attribute this finding to the timing of the examination relative to the abuse and the difficulties of conducting comparative studies in this area. Sexual abuse does not usually leave lasting traces and damage to the anogenital area is reported to heal quickly (De Laar and Lagro-Janssen 2009). However, it is important to note that children and young people presenting with suspected child sexual abuse should be assessed by those with specialist expertise and access to a colposcope. Where possible children and young people presenting as possible victims of sexual abuse should be given a choice as to the gender of their examiner. Repeated examinations of this intimate nature may be viewed as being abusive in themselves. In my experience, nurses and midwives have had to intervene to advocate for protecting the child from an inexperienced, but concerned, clinician who is keen to make a 'diagnosis'. An exception to this state of affairs would be in the rare cases where urgent medical attention may be required.

Anogenital signs and symptoms that are suggestive of child sexual abuse include bruising, laceration, swelling or abrasion in the absence of a suitable explanation, persistent soreness and bleeding or discharge without medical explanation and with associated behavioural or emotional change. The guidelines tackle the controversial issue of the 'reflex anal dilatation' (RAD) test[2] and conclude that this should be undertaken by an experienced professional, rather than a front-line health care practitioner (NCCWCH 2009).

Practice point

Nelson (2009) points out that people who have been sexually abused as children may be reluctant to present for health care and avoid examinations of sensitive parts of their bodies (e.g. dentistry or gynaecology). This can result in additional or preventable health problems for them and, in the case of pregnancy, unborn babies too.

The effects of child sexual abuse

Not surprisingly, child sexual abuse can have a serious and enduring impact on the physical, emotional and sexual health of individuals across their lifespan. In summarizing the research on the impact of this form of maltreatment, *Working Together* (HM Government 2010: 260) notes that this may include disturbed behaviour such as 'self-harm, inappropriate sexualised behaviour, sexually abusive behaviour, depression and a loss of self-esteem'.

The severity of the impact is reported to increase with the length and extensiveness of the abuse, the age of the child, the relationship of the abuser with the child, and the degree of premeditation, threat, coercion and unusual or sadistic elements.

Myers *et al.* (2002) provide a detailed summary of the research findings on the effects of child sexual abuse. They suggest that two decades of research into the outcomes for those who have been sexually abused as children has found a 'wide range of psychological and interpersonal problems' (p. 59). The authors link their findings to the fact that this form of abuse is frightening, painful and confusing, and that it induces shame and bewilderment. Fundamentally, the authors propose that sexual abuse leads to responses in childhood that interfere with normal developmental processes and they summarize the effects on children and young people in terms of causing emotional distress

---

[2]See Campbell (1988) for an excellent review of the events of 1987, in which there was widespread public misperception of miscarriages of justice in relation to diagnoses of child sexual abuse and vilification of paediatricians and other professionals working in the child protection field.

and dysfunction, post-traumatic stress, behavioural problems, interpersonal consequences and cognitive difficulties. However, they do acknowledge that much of the research that they reviewed concerned clinical, rather than population, samples and thus may not be generalizable. Myers *et al.* also report on a number of studies that have considered the longer-term outcomes for children who have been sexually abused and found that these include depression, suicide, anxiety, poor relationships, running away from home, substance misuse, eating disorders, abnormal sexual behaviour and poor achievement at school.

Practice question

Given the evidence that suggests that the reactions of practitioners to a child or young person who discloses sexual abuse have an impact on the child's ability to cope, how can you ensure that you (and members of your team) are receptive, believing and responsive to the need for protection of children who have been sexually abused?

Importantly, while Myers *et al.* acknowledge that there were few follow-up studies of child victims of sexual abuse, those that had been undertaken reported that there was only a limited evidence of improvement in these adverse effects over time and that some children had significant continuing symptomatology into adulthood, where a history of childhood sexual abuse was recognized to constitute a 'major risk factor for a variety of problems in adult life' (Myers *et al.* 2002: 61). Many of the difficulties reported are an extension of those reported in childhood and include psychological problems such as:

- depression;
- suicidal behaviours anxiety;
- self-harm (or violence to others);
- dissociation;[3]
- low self-esteem;
- eating disorders;
- substance misuse.

The authors also found that relationship problems and sexual dysfunction, including multiple partners and unsafe sexual practices, are reported as being more commonly experienced by adult survivors of sexual abuse.

Given the range of adverse outcomes highlighted above, it is very likely that adult survivors of sexual abuse will feature within patient and client groups in a variety of settings, including adult mental health services. Nurses and midwives thus need to be open, responsive and compassionate and know how to access additional support for this group of people.

---

[3]Dissociation is a term used to describe a disconnection of thoughts, feelings, sensations and memories that may result in the diagnosis of a dissociation disorder (e.g. amnesia).

Finally, it is worth concluding this section with a more optimistic finding on the apparently common concern that there is a high risk of those who were sexually abused as children becoming perpetrators themselves in their adult life. This is not borne out in reality and a consistent message for practice is that timely and responsive interventions to child sexual abuse that promote emotional and cognitive resolution may improve the chances of a positive outcome in later life.

Practice point

It would be quite wrong to suggest that most children who are sexually abused inevitably go on to become abusers themselves.

HM Government (2010: 260)

The following case scenarios describe three different presentations of sexual abuse. Links are made to the evidence base for practice and to the statutory guidance. In each case the actions of the nurse are described in terms of best practice.

Case 1: Marnie – a 14-year-old at risk

Marnie, who presents at a contraception and sexual health outreach clinic for young people, looks somewhat older than her 14 years. She has booked in to see Celine, the lead nurse, and is requesting a pregnancy test. Marnie is accompanied by her friend Jo, who is also 14 years of age. Jo states that she would also like to speak to the nurse. The girls have been dropped off at the clinic by an older woman, who waits outside in her car.

Practice question

How should the statutory guidance in relation to sexually active young people influence Celine's assessment of Marnie and Jo's potential child protection needs?

Both girls are extremely reluctant to disclose details of their circumstances. Marnie will not provide details of any sexual partners. When asked about school and family life she becomes evasive; she has not been attending school very often recently and her family background sounds somewhat chaotic and disruptive. There are reports of disputes with neighbours, several managed moves and recent 'sofa-surfing' with Jo and other friends. Celine is concerned about the fact that the girls appear tired and drawn. She wonders if they have been using substances, including alcohol. There is a strong smell of cigarettes. Celine explains that she will provide contraceptive and sexual health advice to the girls, including the pregnancy test for Marnie. However, she also gently explains that her concerns about their situation, and in particular their safety, mean that she will need to make a referral to children's social care service. While assuring a level of confidentiality about the advice and treatment that is offered, Celine also asks the girls for more details of their parents, who need to be informed of the situation in relation to their safety and the referral to children's social care. The concern here is that the girls are being subjected to sexual exploitation. The older woman in the car outside is not a relative.

Practice point

Concerns about confidentiality are frequently cited as a reason that prevents young people from accessing contraception and sexual health advice and treatment. If information has to be shared (as in this case), it is important to seek consent, explain why information needs to be shared, and share only what is necessary and proportionate. Decisions about information-sharing (even in cases where the decision is not to share) must always be carefully documented.

In this case, if the girls refuse to give consent, this can be overridden because taking action would be considered to be in their best interest. This should also be explained to them.

Sexual exploitation as a form of child sexual abuse

Sexual exploitation of children and young people is a form of child sexual abuse. The need to protect children from sexual exploitation is explicitly recognized in the United Nations Convention on the Rights of the Child 1989 (see Chapter 1). It is a global issue and one that the UK has sought to address through a range of additional child protection guidance. The sexual exploitation of children is largely a hidden problem, with no true indication of prevalence. Various charities and voluntary agencies (for example Barnardo's) are undertaking projects across the UK to assess the scale of this form of abuse and try and prevent children and young people falling prey to those who promise a range of gifts and lifestyles in return for sexual favours.

In the past the notion of sexual exploitation of children was largely referred to as 'child prostitution'; however, this label fails to recognize that the child or young person is essentially being abused by those who hold power over them. This is an issue that needs to be framed within a children's rights framework and, in particular, the protective rights of children and young people. The safety and well-being of the child must be at the centre of the multi-agency response; they are victims and their behaviour should not be criminalized.

In supplementary guidance to *Working Together* the following definition of sexual exploitation is given:

Sexual exploitation of children and young people under 18 involves exploitative situations, contexts and relationships where young people (or a third person or persons) receive 'something' (e.g. food, accommodation, drugs, alcohol, cigarettes, affection, gifts, money) as a result of them performing, and/or another or others performing on them, sexual activities. Child sexual exploitation can occur through the use of technology without the child's immediate recognition; for example being persuaded to post sexual images on the Internet/mobile phones without immediate payment or gain. In all cases, those exploiting the child/young person have power over them by virtue of their age, gender, intellect, physical strength and/or economic or other resources. Violence, coercion and intimidation are common, involvement in exploitative relationships being characterised in the main by the child or young person's limited availability of choice resulting from their social/economic and/or emotional vulnerability.

(HM Government 2009: 9)

The above guidance provides a very useful overview of the key issues and is recommended as key reading for those who work with young people, especially in school health, contraception and sexual health services, child and adolescent mental health services (CAMHS), urgent care centres and emergency departments.

Practice point

Sexual activity at a young age is a very strong indicator of risks to the welfare of a young person and, possibly, other young people too.

Although the risk of sexual exploitation applies to any child or young person, certain groups, such as those with a history of maltreatment or other adverse events in their childhood, children in care, those who truant from school or run away from home, immigrants and those with learning difficulties are reported to be at greater risk. There are also links with forced marriage.[4] Boys as well as girls are targeted and for some the activity can lead to confusion of sexual orientation (HM Government 2009). In contrast with a commonly held view of prostitutes offering their wares on street corners, children and young people who are subject to sexual exploitation are usually hidden from view. It is shocking to find that those organizing the abuse may include family members, as well as other adults. The response to the sexual exploitation of children adds additional challenges to Local Safeguarding Children Board (LSCB) partners, including health services, in that this form of abuse crosses geographical boundaries, as well as UK borders. Some of the victims have been found to have been trafficked for the purposes of sexual exploitation (see also HM Government 2008d). The use of technology, such as the internet and mobile telephones, adds another important dimension.

---

[4]Forced marriage is when one or both partners are married without their consent. For help and advice on this matter see www.fco.gov.uk/en/travel-and-living-abroad/when-things-go-wrong/forced-marriage.

The outcomes for children and young people who have been sexually exploited can be extremely poor, and have been linked to long-term physical, psychological and sexual harm (HM Government 2009). For some individuals it can lead to the loss of their life, either through being murdered or by suicide. Other consequences are reported to include:

- unwanted pregnancy;
- sexually transmitted infections, including human immunodeficiency virus (HIV);
- relationship difficulties;
- feeling of worthlessness leading to self-harm and eating disorders;
- substance misuse;
- entering a life of prostitution.

It is therefore paramount that any concerns that a child or young person may be being sexually exploited are shared and actions are taken to safeguard them from further harm. The challenge in a number of cases is that a child may not recognize themselves as being a victim (HM Government 2009).

Practice point

Sexual exploitation of children and young people is a criminal activity. Information-sharing is vital. Nurses and midwives are protected in sharing information if they have concerns about harm to an individual, even in the absence of consent. The sharing of such information is supported by the government guidance highlighted in Chapter 1 (HM Government 2008b) and also by the Nursing and Midwifery Council (NMC) *Code* (2008), which states that practitioners must disclose information if they believe a person to be at risk of harm, in line with the law of the country in which they are practising.

Case 1 continued

Celine obtains as much information as possible from the girls. After discussing the concerns with her manager, and having also sought some additional advice from the named nurse safeguarding children, she makes a referral to children's social care. The next actions will be to plan for the immediate safety of the girls. If the girls' parents cannot be contacted, then police protection (see Chapter 3) may be sought. In ensuring the safety and protection of these young people, Celine's actions may also lead to timely intervention in preventing sexual abuse and exploitation of others. Information shared is proportionate, but a positive pregnancy test would have additional implications in terms of the need to provide advice and to support a decision for Marnie to either seek a termination of pregnancy (at the earliest opportunity) or to refer to a midwife for care in pregnancy and delivery. Chapter 2 highlights the implications of teenage pregnancy.

> **Markers of best practice: the role of the sexual health nurse**
>
> In making her assessment of the sexual health needs of Marnie (and her friend), Celine recognizes two extremely vulnerable young people. Although it is Marnie who is presenting for health care, Jo's needs are also assessed as evident.
>
> In line with statutory guidance on working with sexually active young people, Celine considers that the following points drawn from the *Working Together* guidance (HM Government 2010: 142) may apply and thus support the actions that she takes to safeguard the girls from possible significant harm:
>
> - the age of the girls (14 years);
> - the limited information that they provided about their circumstances;
> - that there may be an age or power imbalance with a sexual partner;
> - that they may be being groomed;
> - that there may be signs of coercion or bribery;
> - the fact that the girls were withdrawn and anxious;
> - the possible misuse of substances;
> - the secrecy surrounding any sexual partner and the identity of the accompanying woman.
>
> Celine completes clear, contemporaneous records of the events and her actions, with particular regard to her judgement of the possibility of significant harm and information-sharing with children's social care (NMC 2009).

Case 2: Jodie — a child with disabilities who is subject to a child protection plan

The second case study in this chapter concerns the complexities of the care of a child with a progressive disability, who is also subject to a child protection plan under the category of risk of sexual abuse. Jodie, who is 10 years of age, suffers from a rare inherited condition called Sanfilippo syndrome, one of a group of enzyme deficiency conditions known as the mucopolysaccharide diseases.[5] Although sufferers from this group of conditions display few symptoms as babies, the disease causes progressive cellular damage and increasing levels of disability. The disease is usually described as having three phases: the first phase, in early childhood, is characterized by the onset of developmental delay (e.g. delayed speech and behavioural difficulties); the second phase, in middle childhood, is characterized by increasingly active and challenging behaviour (such as sleep disturbance and aggressive behaviour); and the third phase, from

---

[5] See www.mpssociety.co.uk/index.php?page=sanfilippo-disease.

the age of about 10 years, is characterized by increasing neurological and motor difficulties, with a life expectancy of the late teens. Recently, arrangements have been made for Jodie to attend the local children's hospice for respite care. Marcus, a learning disability nurse, works within the hospice and also provides an outreach service to help to ensure joined-up care and family involvement.

Caring for a child with this condition is fraught with emotional and practical challenges. Jodie's stepfather and mother, Simon and Natasha, who have three other younger children, have recently separated following an extensive period of unhappiness. In addition to the stress caused by caring for a child with a progressive and life-limiting disability, the couple have had to come to terms with an incident involving Damian, Simon's teenage son from an earlier relationship, who was suspected of sexually abusing Jodie while baby-sitting for the family. As a result of this, Jodie and her siblings are subject to a formal child protection plan (HM Government 2010).

Child maltreatment and children with disabilities

There has been growing evidence that children and young people who are disabled are likely to be at a three-fold greater risk of child maltreatment when compared with their non-disabled peers, yet they are under-represented in safeguarding children systems. This state of affairs has led to the production of a further volume of supplementary guidance to *Working Together* (HM Government 2010) that specifically considers the need for LSCBs and their partner agencies to address the problem and to ensure that this group of children are appropriately, and proactively, safeguarded from harm (Murray and Osborne 2009). The guidance, which is recommended reading for those involved in the care of children with disabilities and their families, specifically notes that:

> Disabled children and young people should be seen as children first. Having a disability should not and must not mask or deter an appropriate enquiry where there are child protection concerns. This premise is relevant to all those involved with disabled children and is *particularly relevant to health care workers* given the key role they play and their close involvement with many disabled children and their families.
>
> Murray and Osborne (2009: 13, emphasis added)

There are several possible reasons for the greater risk of maltreatment for children with disabilities. At a societal level people with disabilities may suffer from negative attitudes, prejudice, discrimination and unequal access to goods and services. They are also more likely to suffer from bullying. The poorer outcomes for disabled children reflect reduced educational, social and recreational opportunities, an increased likelihood of poverty and social exclusion, as well as a greater chance of family breakdown and being a child in care. As individuals, children with disabilities may face the challenge of speech, language and communication difficulties. Equally, those caring for them may not have learned the skills of communicating in a different way (e.g. signing or the use of communication boards).

Practice question

Do you, and/or others in your area of practice have the ability to communicate differently with those with speech, language or communication difficulties?

Because of their disability, this group of children and young people may be dependent on others (i.e. parents and carers) for support with activities of daily living, including intimate care. Furthermore, it is important to note that professionals and others working with families with a disabled child or young person can develop very intensive relationships with parents, and over-identify with them, with the result that it becomes difficult both to acknowledge, and to respond to, concerns about the child's safety and well-being. Although this chapter concerns the sexual abuse of children and young people, it is timely to reinforce the message that children and young people with disabilities are more likely to suffer from all forms of maltreatment: physical abuse, emotional abuse, sexual abuse and neglect. However, in relation to sexual abuse, Murray and Osborne (2009) make some noteworthy points in relation to the blocks that can prevent professionals from being open to the possibility of this form of abuse. These include the denial of the child or young person's sexuality and confusing behaviours that may indicate sexual abuse with those associated with the disability.

The child protection plan

As we noted in Chapter 4, the decision at an initial child protection conference (ICPC) to make a child or young person subject to a formal child protection plan (previously known as 'being on the child protection register') is determined by the questions of whether they have suffered significant harm, and whether or not they are likely to be at risk of suffering significant harm in the future. The local authority takes responsibility for holding and updating a list of children and young people who are subject to a child protection plan. Agencies can contact children's social care both in office hours and via out of hours services to make enquiries as to whether or not children and young people are subject to a plan in cases where this information is seen to be vital to informing the delivery of care (e.g. emergency departments).

The primary purposes of a child protection plan are to 'prevent the child suffering harm or a recurrence of harm in the future and to promote the child's welfare' (HM Government 2010: 167). The child protection plan outlines an overall aim, as well as a number of short- and long-term actions and objectives for professionals and the family, in order to reduce the likelihood of further harm. Arrangements are then put in place to monitor the safety and well-being of the child (or children) and the compliance with the plan. The format of the plan draws on *The Child's Plan* (DH 2003) which was introduced to ensure holistic and child-centred care for those with additional safeguarding needs.

A child protection plan is a formal document in which the following are agreed and recorded:

- actions to be undertaken/services to be provided;
- frequency/length of service;
- person/agency responsible;
- date of commencement;
- planned outcomes/progress to be achieved by next review.

There should be a clear contingency for failures to deliver or achieve actions and objectives and to escalate concerns, if necessary. By signing up to the child protection plan, families are providing a written agreement to work together with professionals to safeguard and promote the welfare of their child.

Child protection plans are monitored (and, if necessary, refined) by a 'core group' comprising the allocated social worker, the child or young person (if appropriate), the parents or carers (and possibly other family members) and the key professionals involved with the child and family. The responsibility for chairing the core group and managing the plan sits with the lead statutory body: either children's social care or, in some areas, the National Society for the Prevention of Cruelty to Children (NSPCC). Accountability for delivering the plan rests with all the members of the core group, including the family. The child and family should be fully informed as to the reasons and purpose of the child protection plan; advice also needs to be provided on access to advocacy and support services for them. Meetings of the core group normally take place on a six-weekly basis, between the date of the ICPC and the review child protection conferences (see Chapter 6). It is also important that the core group have a contingency plan, which should be followed if circumstances change and require action.

Jodie's child protection plan

In Jodie's (and her siblings') case, the core group comprises Marcus, as the health professional who has the most frequent contact with the family, along with:

- Jodie's mother and an aunt;
- the lead social worker (who will be the 'key worker');
- a social worker from the children with disabilities team;
- the designated officer for safeguarding children (DOSC) from Jodie's special school;
- a school nurse;
- a health visitor and an early years worker.[6]

A child protection plan will be drawn up for each of the children. The plan for Jodie includes an outline of her health and developmental needs.

---

[6]These professionals have a role with Jodie's siblings.

Jodie's child protection plan

Action	Person/agency responsible	Outcomes
There will be two-weekly planned joint visits to monitor Jodie's well-being	Key worker, children's social care and learning disability nurse, health provider	Jodie's welfare will be safeguarded and promoted
There will be alternate-week unannounced visits to assess Jodie's well-being and her parents' compliance with the requirements of the plan	Key worker, children's social care	Parents will comply with the child protection plan Jodie's welfare will be safeguarded and promoted
Jodie will receive an enhanced package of care that includes the delivery of a 'safe-touch' programme by [date]	School nurse, health provider and DOSC, special school	Jodie will have an awareness of her right to physical integrity and an enhanced ability to protect herself
Damian's contact with Jodie will be supervised at all times	Parents and aunt to Jodie, mother to Damian	Jodie will be protected from further risk of sexual abuse
The frequency of provision of respite care to be reviewed	Key worker, social worker, disability team and parents	Respite care provided is proportionate to Jodie's needs and the needs of the family at a time of additional stress
Staff at the hospice are aware of the child protection plan	Key worker and hospice staff	Staff are enabled to be vigilant regarding any additional concerns about Jodie's safety and well-being

The over-arching aim of the child protection plan is to ensure that Jodie and her siblings do not suffer future harm, and a range of measures are put in place, including asking the family not to allow Damian to have unsupervised access to the children. Key to the core group, Marcus is able to provide advice on Jodie's condition, her health and developmental needs and assist other professionals in communicating with her. This includes supporting professionals who are helping Jodie in understanding 'safe touch'. Marcus is supported in his safeguarding role by his manager and the community health service provider organization's named nurse safeguarding children. The plan will be monitored and reviewed by the core group and progress reported to the review child protection conference.

> **Practice point**
>
> Marcus should seek regular child protection supervision to ensure that he is able to remain focused on the need to safeguard and promote the welfare of Jodie and her siblings. Given the complexity of the family situation, and a genuine feeling of compassion for Natasha and Simon, it is important that the children's needs and interests are placed at the centre of his assessments and interventions.

Case 2 continued

In becoming involved in Jodie's case, Marcus finds himself questioning the safeguarding children knowledge and understanding of the children's hospice staff, some of whom have found it difficult to acknowledge the abuse that has taken place. He is also concerned to find that the organization's internal safeguarding children policy and procedures document appears to be quite superficial. While the document provides guidance on what to do if there are concerns that a child is being maltreated, as well as details of how to seek further advice and make a referral to the local children's social care department, it is disappointingly 'thin' on the particular risks of maltreatment faced by children and young people with disabilities. Marcus believes that this is an important omission because these children are a group who make up an increasingly large proportion of the children and families in their care.

Furthermore, Marcus' experiences of the child protection processes surrounding Jodie and her family have made him reflect on the readiness and ability of the LSCB's partners to recognize and respond to concerns that a child with a disability is being harmed. He discovers that there are no statistics available on the number of disabled children subject to a child protection plan, a factor that he believes could be discriminatory. Marcus is also aware that for many families with disabled young people facing transition to adult services, including residential care, there is a need to ensure that safeguarding adult policies and procedures are also in place locally. Drawing on the evidence base for practice and policy outlined by Murray and Osborne (2009) and with the support of his manager, the LSCB chair and the named nurse, Marcus proposes the following objectives at his annual appraisal and review.

- To become the named safeguarding lead for the children's hospice.
- To revise and update the organization's internal safeguarding children policy and procedures.

- To undertake to develop a programme of in-house safeguarding children training and to ensure that those staff requiring 'Group Three' training[7] are able to access the inter-agency safeguarding training provided by the LSCB and children's Trust.
- To support the LSCB chair in working with a 'task and finish' group to develop an inter-agency protocol to support good safeguarding children practice for disabled children and young people across local partners.
- To review the local arrangements for safeguarding adults to ensure that the needs of adults with disabilities are explicitly recognized and monitored.

Markers of good practice: the role of the learning disability nurse

Marcus' role in safeguarding Jodie and her family is both to provide ongoing care and support, and also to act as an advocate and expert. His skills and knowledge are vital to ensure that the child protection plan achieves its aims, objectives and actions to safeguard and promote the welfare of all the children in the family.

He is a member of the core group and will ensure that he prioritizes attendance and produces reports, which he shares with the family prior to any meetings. He will also attend the review child protection conference.

Marcus also recognizes the potential for improvements to safeguarding children, young people and adults with disabilities and takes action to influence and transform practice. In doing so he is practising within his professional remit to work with others to protect and promote the health and well being of the wider community (NMC 2009b).

Case 3: Stewart – an adult client who discloses activity that is linked with child sexual abuse

Stewart is a 38-year-old divorced father of two, who suffers from recurrent manic depression. He is cared for by a community mental health team led by Georgiou, a registered nurse (mental health). Stewart is currently unemployed, has major debt issues and has recently admitted to 'drinking [alcohol] to excess'. This is having a big impact on his treatment and his present state of mental and physical health. Georgiou, who has taken on the role of mental health care coordinator, undertakes a home visit to make an assessment. Stewart presents as pale, tearful and anxious, and explains that his estranged ex-wife has sought to further reduce his contact with his children. During the visit Stewart admits that he is accessing the internet on a regular basis to watch child pornography – for which he has to pay – and that he is also passing on images to others who indulge in this activity. Stewart begs Georgiou not to

---

[7] See *Working Together* (HM Government 2010), Chapter 4, for more details.

record or share this information with anyone else, adding that it has been shared by him in strict confidence.

> **Practice question**
>
> Should Georgiou respect his client's right to confidentiality?

Child abuse and information and communication technology

Working Together (HM Government 2010) includes non-statutory practice guidance on child abuse and information and communication technology (ICT).[8] Here it is recognized that the internet has become a 'significant tool in the distribution of indecent photographs/pseudo photographs of children' (p. 315). Crucially, the guidance also recognizes that there is evidence to support the fact that people found in possession of such images are likely to be involved directly in child abuse. The Internet Watch Foundation[9] provides comprehensive details of the legislation that applies in such cases. In particular, the Sexual Offences Act 1978 (England and Wales) recognizes that it is an offence to take, permit to be taken, make, possess, show, distribute or advertise indecent images of children in the UK.

Many parents and carers express concerns about children and young people's use of the internet and other forms of ICT. Sponsored by the Child Exploitation and Online Protection Centre (CEOP), the 'ThinkUKnow'[10] website offers tailored guidance for professionals, parents and children themselves on protection from sexual exploitation (both on- and off-line) and also cyberbullying. The CEOP site has a facility to access help and advice and make reports about online activity that may indicate crimes against children and young people.

Case 3 continued

Georgiou contacts his line manager for advice and support in reporting the matter to the police. Given the fact that his concerns would meet the threshold for 'public interest', details of Stewart's disclosure of accessing child pornography are passed to the local police child abuse referral unit.

Although Stewart has requested his right to confidentiality in this matter, Georgiou has taken the correct decision in reporting the disclosure to the police. This apparent breach of confidentiality meets the NMC *Code* (2008) requirement that information is shared because it is believed that someone

---

[8]See HM Government (2010), Part 2, Chapters 9–12.
[9]See www.iwf.org.uk.
[10]See www.thinkuknow.co.uk.

is at risk of harm. The sharing of information without consent would also be supported by the information-sharing guidance as being in the public interest. However, in most cases it is best practice to inform the client that information will be shared, what will be shared, with whom, and the reasons for doing so. In their enquiries, the police will have to consider Stewart's access to children, including his own. There may be a need for them to work with children's social care services to initiate a Section 47 investigation as it is possible that Stewart's children have been party to watching the pornography or even been caught up in the production of images. Stewart is currently not in work, but if his employment or any volunteering activities involved working with children and young people (e.g. Scout leader), then this would have to be addressed.

Markers of best practice: the role of the mental health nurse

Before the establishment of any therapeutic relationship, it is advisable to set out with the client the professional boundaries, duties and responsibilities in relation to confidentiality. Georgiou recognizes that he has to share information with the police following the disclosure. He seeks support from his line manager, but equally could have approached his organization's safeguarding children leads.

Georgiou completes clear, contemporaneous records of the events and his actions, with particular regard to the admission of criminal activity that was causing harm to others and his decision to share information with the police (NMC 2009b).

Summary

This chapter has considered child sexual abuse. As noted in the statutory definition, sexual abuse may involve physical contact or non-contact activities such as involving the child in looking at sexual images or grooming in preparation for abuse. An important message is that children may not be aware at the time that what is happening to them is abusive. Three scenarios have been presented. The first concerned Marnie and her friend Jo and the possibility that they were experiencing sexual abuse through sexual exploitation. The second scenario concerned Jodie, who has a progressive and life-limiting condition and a range of disabilities that have made her vulnerable to sexual abuse. The third scenario demonstrated the need to take action in informing the police following a disclosure by an adult mental health services client that they were accessing child pornography online. The nursing staff involved in these fictitious scenarios were a sexual health nurse, a learning disabilities nurse and an adult mental health nurse. A range of safeguarding actions were described. The scenarios demonstrate the importance of information-sharing, as well as the very positive actions that nurses and midwives can take in ensuring the safety and well-being of individual clients or patients, their families and communities.

Key points

- Sexual abuse of children is common: 16 per cent of children and young people in one survey reported sexually abusive experiences in their childhood.
- Children and young people who are sexually abused experience difficulty in telling their story. Victims are not always aware that what is happening to them is abusive.
- The effects of child sexual abuse are enduring and may be lifelong.
- Children who are disabled have a three-fold risk of being abused, but are under-represented in safeguarding systems.
- Confidentiality in a patient–client relationship is *not* absolute; this should be explained to clients at the outset of any therapeutic relationship.
- In the case of Stewart, the 'public interest' would be served by reporting his online activity to the police.

6 Neglect

Learning outcomes

This chapter will help you to:

- Understand the features of neglect as a form of child maltreatment.
- Identify indicators that may be associated with neglect.
- Appreciate the challenges to recognizing and responding to neglect in practice.
- Make a professional contribution to a child protection review conference, including supporting a decision to remove children's names from being subject to a formal child protection plan.

Introduction

Nurses and midwives working with children, young people and their families may encounter neglect in the course of their practice. As with emotional abuse, context, rather than a specific event, underpins a recognition of this form of maltreatment, although it frequently co-exists with other forms of child maltreatment. Drawing on the statutory guidance we begin by defining what is meant by 'neglect' and outlining some of the key indicators of concern. Throughout the chapter links are made to the evidence base for practice, as well as to safeguarding and child protection policy and procedures. Once again, three case scenarios are presented. These illustrate examples of child neglect and the practice implications for nurses, midwives and health visitors. The cases are fictitious, but based on reality.

- Case 1: Jack, a newborn baby, is at risk of neglect because of his mother's lifestyle. Christina, a community midwife, is anxious about his future well-being.
- Case 2: 18-month-old twins Courtney and Kendra presented at 9 months with 'faltering growth' and other physical indicators of neglect. They have subsequently been subject to a child protection plan and the case is due to be reviewed. Amanda, the health visitor, will attend the child protection review conference.

- Case 3: Riley, aged 4 years, was admitted to a paediatric intensive care unit with respiratory depression after accidentally ingesting one of his father's suboxone tablets. Molly, a substance misuse practitioner, has been supporting an investigation into the case.

It is important for nurses and midwives to understand the seriousness of neglect and to be vigilant. Neglect is an important, and preventable, cause of health and developmental difficulties for children. It is currently the most common reason for children to be made subject to a child protection plan. We begin by defining neglect.

Neglect

Neglect is a form of child maltreatment that is multi-faceted. It can also occur alongside other forms of abuse. Some of the child protection literature makes reference to 'emotional neglect' as well as 'physical neglect', but these often co-exist and both are subsumed within the statutory guidance's definition of neglect:

Neglect is the persistent failure to meet a child's basic physical and/or psychological needs, likely to result in the serious impairment of the child's health or development. Neglect may occur during pregnancy as a result of maternal substance abuse. Once a child is born, neglect may involve a parent or carer failing to:

- provide adequate food, clothing and shelter (including exclusion from home or abandonment);
- protect a child from physical and emotional harm or danger;
- ensure adequate supervision (including the use of inadequate care-givers); or
- ensure access to appropriate medical care or treatment.

It may also include neglect of, or unresponsiveness to, a child's basic emotional needs.

(HM Government 2010: 39)

Neglect can impact on the health and development of children and young people at a number of levels. According to Gilbert *et al.* (2008) neglect is at least as damaging as physical or sexual abuse. Moreover, Brandon *et al.* (2009) found that it is increasingly being recognized as an underlying factor in the cases that become subject to a serious case review, including those concerning adolescent suicide and self-harm. An essential theme of neglect is 'omission' or 'absence of care'. This means that those who practice in settings where there is an ongoing relationship with a family, especially where there is a requirement to undertake home visits, may be best placed to recognize situations where there is neglect of children's health and developmental needs. However, in these situations, there is also the ever present danger of practitioners becoming accustomed to sub-optimal care, especially where families are living in poor material circumstances where the risk of neglect is, not surprisingly, somewhat greater. In their classic text, Dingwall *et al.* (1983) refer to the 'rule of optimism' whereby professionals are drawn to find the most positive explanation for what is essentially neglectful parenting. This means that there can be a concomitant failure to recognize and respond to neglect in a timely manner. In all cases, it is the daily lived experiences of the child or young person that should be at the centre of any assessment and referral for concerns about neglect.

Prevalence of neglect

The number of children and young people who are subject to a child protection plan under the category of neglect has been rising in recent years, and now represents the largest proportion of those with a plan, at around 45 per cent of the total (DCSF 2009). The reasons for this could be that there is a genuine increase in neglect, or that practitioners are getting better at recognizing and responding to situations in which children's health and development are neglected. This is borne out by Gardner (2008), who interviewed 100 practitioners from across the spectrum of agencies who work with children. The sample included school nurses and health visitors, as well as a range of practitioners from other disciplines. Gardner found a good general awareness of neglect in her sample, with some practitioners reporting that a degree of child neglect was a feature in as many as 80 per cent of the families in their caseloads.

Practice point

Disabled children, and those with a chronic illness, are noted to be at particular risk of neglect. This may be due to family circumstance, service provision or society's attitudes to disability (RCPCH 2006).[1]

Cawson *et al.*'s (2000) seminal study sought to describe the features and the scale of child neglect in the UK, alongside other forms of child maltreatment. Here neglect is portrayed in terms of the absence of physical care at home and/or the absence of appropriate supervision. A further delineation between what may be considered to be 'serious absence' and what may be considered to be 'some absence' is made, with neglectful experiences before the age of 12 years being seen to be at the more serious end of the spectrum. The examples include:

- living in dangerous home situations;
- frequent hunger;
- having to wear dirty clothes to school;
- a failure to be taken for medical care when ill;

---

[1]See also Chapter 5.

- being abandoned; and
- having to look after themselves due to a parental drug or alcohol problem.

Neglect that is linked to 'some absence' of physical care is related to experiencing similar issues as those described above, but to a lesser degree (or as an older child and therefore with potentially less impact). The examples here also include failure to attend for routine health care such as dentistry. Absence of supervision is said to include being left alone overnight, the severity of which may be judged according to the age at which this happened. The authors also suggest that being allowed to go unsupervised into a town centre at a young age is indicative of 'some absence' of care.

Using the parameters described above, nearly one-fifth of Cawson *et al.*'s (2000) respondents described their childhood experiences as indicating a degree of neglect, with approximately 1 in 20 of the young adults laying claim to having experienced serious absences of physical care or supervision during their childhood. In almost all cases these neglectful experiences were linked to deficits in parental care, with very few of the respondents in the sample having been cared for outside their family. While this study is frequently lauded for its approach and sampling methodologies, it is reliant on the respondents' ability to recall events across childhood. This means that the experiences that the young adults recalled and reported to the researchers may miss out events that occurred in infancy. This is important because the broader evidence consistently finds that it is the youngest children who are the most vulnerable to abuse and neglect.[2]

The literature on neglect frequently centres on the concept of a 'persistent failure' in care – i.e. that neglect is a relentless ongoing situation in the lives of the children and young people who suffer from this form of maltreatment. However, the Royal College of Paediatrics and Child Health (RCPCH) recognizes that while neglect is usually chronic, there may be times of crisis in the lives of families that lead to *episodic* neglect (RCPCH 2006). The examples given here include divorce or parental mental illness, such as depression. The RCPCH also reminds readers that neglect can occur in middle-class families – for instance, children left 'home alone' or unattended while parents are working.

Practice question

What would you do if you were undertaking a home visit and found a child under the age of 12 years 'home alone'?

Agreeing what is, and what is not, child neglect can be challenging. In my previous safeguarding children text (Powell 2007), I drew attention to the ostensibly controversial work by Golden *et al.* (2003) who took the view

[2]Although there has been a recent attempt to more accurately represent the risk and impact of neglect in adolescence (Stein *et al.* 2009).

that the use of the term 'neglect' was somewhat mild. The authors' concerns were that the use of the concept suggested a *non-deliberate* failure to meet the needs of children through stress, competing priorities, lack of education and socioeconomic deprivation. Indeed, they argue that most parents will be guilty of neglect at some point, adding that it might actually be beneficial for children and young people's development into adulthood to experience not having all their needs met fully at all times.

By noting that in comparison with other forms of abuse neglect does not 'fit' with statutory procedures (that are designed to deal with an incident rather than a context) Golden *et al.* (2003) questioned the usefulness of a child protection approach for neglect. 'Mothers' [*sic*], they add, who are struggling with the challenges of parenting and adverse social and financial circumstances, are often aware that the care they are providing is not as good as it should be, but are less aware of the impact of this care on the child. In a similar vein, Gardner (2008) describes the concerns that many professionals have that in raising questions of neglect within families they may be seen to be blaming parents who are not 'intentionally abusive'.

Compared with other forms of child maltreatment, neglect is evidently difficult to define and address. This is because it is clearly open to broader influences, heavily reliant on professional judgement and prone to discrepant parental interpretation. These factors are borne out in the next section that seeks to outline indicators of possible neglect.

Indicators of child neglect

One of the problems in identifying neglect as a form of child maltreatment is that any assessment will be somewhat subjective. The statutory guidance, for instance, uses terminology such as 'adequate' and 'persistent' in its definition. There are likely to be differences of opinion as to the interpretation of these terms and thus differences in agreement between agencies on the threshold for a level of neglect that requires compulsory intervention in family life. A further difficulty is that some of the indicators of neglect may have other causes than the adequacy of parenting, an assessment of which is nevertheless important. A good example of this is developmental delay (Daniel *et al.* 2009).

Judgements are inevitably value-laden and based on both personal and professional experiences. Middle-class health professionals can find themselves benchmarking families that they meet in the course of their work with their own experiences of child-rearing and child care (i.e. their expectations of parents and parenting are too high). Equally, they can also make somewhat benevolent allowances for struggling or needy parents and thus fail to recognize that the sub-optimal parenting they are witnessing is actually overt neglect of a child.

The guidelines produced by the National Institute for Health and Clinical Excellence (NICE) note that there is an ever-present danger that professionals who are working with families with complex problems may use strategies that attempt to empower and support parents/carers, leading to their becoming the primary client, while the risk to the child is accumulating and may go unnoticed (NCCWCH 2009). Again we come back to the importance of considering the daily lived experience of the child or young person and ensuring that assessment and interventions are centred on *their* needs.

The needs and challenges of keeping focused on the well-being of the child demonstrate how the value of high-quality supervision is critical to good practice. The process and benefits of supervision are summed up brilliantly by Burton (2009: 9) who notes that:

> Supervisors can support critical thinking and reflection, helping practitioners to use both their intuitive and analytic reasoning skills, to value and understand the respective contributions of each, and hopefully to achieve a more integrated approach. Supervision sessions should both support and challenge practitioners, helping them to avoid the temptation to slip uncritically into either an analysis skewed by bias and unfounded assumptions, or simply defaulting to the entrenched 'agency view'.

In helping professionals to recognize and respond to neglect, the NICE guidelines echo the themes of failure or absence in parental care already mentioned. They also recognize the challenges of the contextual elements that underpin this form of child maltreatment. Like Golden *et al.* (2003) there is recognition that parents may not always be aware of the impact of their failures in caring for their children:

> Neglect can be conceptualised as a process involving accumulating risk to the child due to a failure to provide or omission rather than actual incidents of abuse. It is a persistent failure to meet the child's or young person's needs that may or may not be wilful.
>
> (NCCWCH 2009: 66)

The importance of benchmarking parental care

In aiming to address the very real difficulties of identifying neglect, as distinct from the effects of material poverty, the NICE guidelines remind practitioners that there is a need to compare what families living with similar constraints manage to achieve, against that achieved by families where neglect is an emerging concern. The universality of the contribution of nurses, midwives and health visitors gives unrivalled opportunities to make these comparisons. The guidelines concede that there is 'no diagnostic gold standard' for neglect (p. 68) but that it should be considered or suspected in the situations outlined in Table 6.1.

An important finding in the literature on neglect is failure to ensure that children and young people access health care, and this is of particular relevance to nurses and midwives and worthy of further analysis at this juncture.

Table 6.1 Consideration and suspicion of neglect

Neglect should be considered	Neglect should be suspected
• Severe or persistent infestations (e.g. head lice or scabies) • Inappropriate clothing and footwear • Faltering growth (failure to thrive) because of lack of adequate or appropriate diet • Explanation of an injury (e.g. a burn, sunburn or ingestion) that suggests a lack of supervision • The presence of an inappropriate caregiver • A failure to administer essential prescribed treatment for a child • A repeated failure to attend follow-up appointments that are essential for their child's well-being • A failure to engage in the Healthy Child Programme (immunizations, health and development reviews and screening)[3] • A failure, despite access, to obtain NHS treatment for a child's dental care	• Child is persistently smelly and dirty • Poor standard of hygiene that is affecting the child's health • Inadequate provision of food • A living environment that is unsafe for the child's developmental standard • Abandonment of a child • A failure to seek medical advice for a child to the extent that the child's health and well-being is compromised, including ongoing pain

Source: adapted from NCCWCH (2009)

Children who are not brought to appointments: an important feature of neglect

One of the consistent findings in the serious case reviews of children and young people who have died, or been seriously harmed through child abuse or neglect, is that there is a history of missed health care appointments (see e.g. Brandon *et al.* 2009). This is also a feature that was found in a more general review that covered all deaths of children aged between 28 days and 18 years over a period of a calendar year (CEMACH 2008). While both documents reflect the fact that death in childhood in the UK is rare (see Chapter 7), they find that there are strong associations with poor social circumstances.

Health care services have traditionally recorded a failure to attend for outpatient clinic appointments as 'did not attend' or 'DNA' for short. It appears to be common practice for the same process for missed appointments in childhood to be followed as it would be for adults – i.e. a second appointment may be sent, but a further failure to attend results in a letter to the GP (and sometimes to the patient) informing them that no further appointments will be sent unless requested by the GP. While acknowledging that missed appointments

---

[3] See DH/DCSF 2009a, 2009b.

are costly to the NHS, and thus the public purse,[4] the issue for children and young people is surely not simply that they *did not attend*, but rather that they *were not brought*.

The problem of missed health care appointments in childhood is raised as a potential child protection concern in the Care Quality Commission (CQC) review of safeguarding children arrangements in the NHS that was published following the death of Peter Connelly (Baby Peter). It is now expected that health services will embed a strategy to address this as part of their safeguarding children policy (CQC 2009). Locally, we have developed a 'was not brought' or 'WNB' guideline that sits alongside the safeguarding children policy. Missing health care appointments can be an important sign that a child is suffering from neglect and may also represent a deteriorating situation within a family, as the extract below from a recent serious case review illustrates:

> Between 1998 and 2008 the children missed a minimum of 129 professional appointments. Undoubtedly, with a family of six children, some of whom had statements of special educational need, there are particular pressures and stresses for parents and a degree of failed appointments would be expected, particularly when the mother was operating as a single parent for periods of time. However, the pattern of failed appointments escalated dramatically during 2007 as relationships with professionals deteriorated. The response to these failures within the agencies was not always actively addressed, or the significance fully understood, and therefore not communicated with partner agencies.
>
> (Birmingham Safeguarding Children Board 2010)

Nevertheless, it is not just a failure to ensure that children and young people are brought to appointments per se. Neglect of health care can also include a failure to respond to advice from health care professionals once health needs in children are recognized (NCCWCH 2009). In some instances there may also be 'disguised compliance' (Reder *et al.* 1993) whereby families appear to be addressing issues that may include failed appointments or school attendance, but in reality are continuing to neglect or abuse their child while seeking to appease professionals with what amounts to a 'smokescreen'.

Disguised compliance is a theme that is frequently reported in the serious case review literature alongside other common themes in relation to parental background and difficulties. This means that while practitioners need to ensure that recognition of, and response to, neglect is focused on the child and their daily lived experiences, it is also important to understand the pressures or difficulties that may lead parents to neglect (or otherwise maltreat) their children. Many of the difficulties that present as parental issues have implications for nurses and midwives in a range of care settings. These are now discussed.

---

[4]See http://news.bbc.co.uk/1/hi/health/8195255.stm (accessed 22 October 2010) where missed appointments are reported to cost the NHS some £600 million per annum.

Parental issues that may lead to neglect of children

The RCPCH (2006) recognizes a number of issues for parents that may impact on what is described as their 'ability or motivation' (p. 44) to meet the needs of their child. In short, and as many readers will recognize, parenting is a selfless activity that not only requires a great deal of energy and resourcefulness, but also for mothers and fathers to be in a position whereby they can place the needs of their children before their own needs. This can be particularly difficult for those whose own experiences of being parented were poor or whose circumstances are not conducive to the enormous demands that parenting entails. Although many parents do manage to parent well, despite their backgrounds or difficulties (see Chapter 4, page 59), the following parental characteristics have been highlighted as increasing the risk for child neglect (RCPCH 2006: 44–5):

- learning disabilities;
- mental health problems;
- substance or alcohol misuse, including binge drinking;
- domestic violence and abuse;
- disability;
- chronic illness;
- unemployment or poverty;
- homelessness;
- young single parents.

Practice question

How can adults with learning disabilities be supported to parent well? On what basis should 'good-enough' parenting by such individuals be assessed?

The issue of parental alcohol misuse and the impact on children has been the subject of a highly publicized review by the Children's Society and Alcohol Concern (Delargy *et al.* 2010). The authors note that parents' drinking can make them unpredictable and less responsive to the needs of their children. This can lead to neglectful situations including poor supervision, a lack of routine and children missing out on celebrations and family events.

The role of nurses and midwives

This chapter opened by considering the defining attributes of neglect. The focus has been largely at an individual or family level with an emphasis on neglect linked to absences in the provision of parental care and/or supervision. It is important now to take a more positive stance and note that neglect is an issue that is 'ripe' for early intervention and prevention at a number of levels. Nurses and midwives, as universal service providers, have a range of opportunities to address the issue and to ensure that children and young people are protected from the devastating effects of neglect. Health visitors, in particular, have been identified as having a key role in reducing inequalities and preventing social exclusion (Queen's Nursing Institute 2007). This can be through the provision of targeted services to children, young people and their parents, or through the delivery of specific programmes such as the family nurse partnership outlined in Chapter 2. However, health visitors' preparation for practice and their core role has long since included an expectation that they will develop the broader skills and knowledge that are required to influence policies affecting health. This could ultimately lead to the political imperative to create a society that better prepares and supports its parents.

The following case scenarios describe three different presentations of neglect. Links are made to the evidence base for practice and to the statutory guidance. In each case the actions of the nurse, midwife and health visitor are described in terms of best practice.

Case 1: Jack — a baby at risk of neglect

Jack, a newborn baby, is the third child of Trinity, who is 23 years old. She was 29 weeks pregnant when she booked for her ante-natal care and attended for two of her remaining appointments. Trinity also saw her community midwife, Christina, at home prior to delivering Jack in the maternity unit at 37 weeks, following a precipitate labour. Jack's birth weight was 2.37 kg, he is deemed to be a healthy infant and Trinity is keen to breast-feed. Jack is already subject to a child protection plan under the category of 'at risk of neglect'. This resulted from plans that were put in place when Jack was an unborn baby and reflects professionals' concerns about his welfare in the context of his parents' past histories and their somewhat chaotic lifestyles.

The background to Jack's child protection plan is that Trinity's two older children were removed from her care as a result of concerns about the impact of her lifestyle and choice of an unsuitable partner, whose own history of violent and controlling behaviour was believed to put the children at considerable risk. The children, who are 6 and 7 years of age, had been subject to inconsistent care and extreme physical punishment. They are currently in the long-term care of non-kinship foster parents. Supervised contact between mother and children has been arranged at a local children's centre, but this has not been entirely successful as Trinity has reported difficulty in arranging the transport needed to get her there.

As a child Trinity herself spent periods of time 'in care' after being abandoned by an alcoholic mother, who has since died. Her father, also called Jack, left the family home when Trinity was 2 years old. Contact with him dwindled over time and has now been lost. Trinity failed to reach her potential at school, in part because she was subject to bullying from others due to her somewhat unkempt appearance and poor clothing, but also because she was often absent due to caring for her mother. There has been something of a re-run of her own childhood in recent years: she has experienced an abusive relationship and desertion, poor housing conditions and removal of her children. Trinity has found that strong lager, bought from the local corner shop, has been helpful in numbing the numerous losses and disappointments in her life. As a result of her experiences, she has few friends and finds it difficult to trust professionals.

Jack is the result of a recent relationship with Joel, who works sporadically as a groundsman in the local park. The pregnancy was unplanned. Joel, who is 28 years of age, has three children by two previous partners. He has been rendered homeless as a result of being 'thrown out' by his last partner and has been sleeping in his van. Joel occasionally smokes cannabis, but does not see this as an issue. The couple report that they are keen to make a new life together and to put their past behind them.

Practice point

When faced with overwhelming information and a feeling of helplessness arising from hearing of the difficult background of their clients, such as the removal of previous children in situations of neglect, practitioners and their managers may adopt what Brandon *et al.* (2008) have termed the 'start again syndrome'. This means that they may fail to ensure that the meaning of the past history is incorporated into present-day assessments. This can result in a failure to adequately protect a child, with sometimes tragic results.

It is clear from the time of the late booking that Trinity is a vulnerable young woman who presents as sullen and difficult to engage. Keen to develop a relationship of trust, midwife Christina arranges to see her at home with her partner although there were two 'no access' visits before she was able to gain access. During the home visit Christina discovers more about the context of the removal of Trinity's two previous children, her violent relationship with their father and her lack of family and social support. During the visit Joel is watchful and silent, as he would be during any contact that Christina has with the family in the coming months. The housing conditions appear to be poor – a small dark room in a privately rented house. Although she feels sorry for Trinity, Christina considers that there are clear risks to the unborn baby arising from the maternal history, the past history of neglect, the removal of two previous children, the substance misuse and the poor engagement of both partners. These concerns are compounded by the late presentation for booking, the missed appointments and the no access visits. In addition, during the home visit Christina sees little in the way of preparedness for a baby. A further concern is the newness of the couple's relationship and the fact that very little information is gleaned in terms of Joel's previous family and social history or the whereabouts of his three children. Fleetingly, Christina also senses an element of quiet control from Joel that she thinks may be an indicator of the possibility of domestic abuse.

Christina informs the couple that she will be discussing their case with a senior midwife and that she will also be asking children's social care to consider undertaking a more detailed assessment and programme of support.

The reasons for her concerns are shared with the couple. There is a passive acceptance of this proposed action and a referral to social care is progressed.

The named midwife

Pre-birth child protection conferences and reviews

Where a core assessment under Section 47 of the Children Act 1989 gives rise to concerns that an unborn child maybe likely to suffer significant harm local authority children's social care may decide to convene an initial child protection conference prior to the child's birth. Such a conference should have the same status, and proceed in the same way, as other initial child protection conferences, including decisions about a child protection plan. Similarly in respect of child protection review conferences. The involvement of midwifery services is vital in such cases.

(HM Government 2010: 181–2)

Christina sought supervision in relation to the safeguarding aspects of the case with the named midwife safeguarding children. According to the statutory guidance, all providers of maternity services are expected to have a named midwife, who will have specific expertise in children's health and development and who, in common with other named professionals, have a role in:

- the promotion of professional practice within their organization;
- the provision of advice and expertise for fellow professionals;
- supporting the organization in its clinical governance role (e.g. through audits);
- ensuring that a training strategy is in place and delivered within their organization.

The role of named midwife should not be confused with that of the supervisor of midwives, whose role is primarily concerned with the safe and effective delivery of midwifery care (NMC 2006). However, arguably the holder of this post should also be skilled and knowledgeable in safeguarding and child protection issues.

Case 1 continued

Following the initial child protection conference, Christina becomes a member of the core group, which works with the family to promote parenting strengths and reduce the risk of neglect. This includes encouraging the couple to engage with professionals and to plan for the safe parenting of Jack. In doing so, Christina works closely with the allocated social worker, including undertaking a joint home visit shortly after Jack's arrival. Christina also ensures that she provides a detailed handover to the health visiting team who will care for the family once they are discharged from midwifery care.

One of the key issues facing the family is that of housing. After her older children were placed in care, and with the threat of serious domestic abuse from her previous partner, Trinity became temporarily homeless. Poor housing is recognized to be a factor in social exclusion and to present a safeguarding risk to children (including risk of accidents and fire). Housing services, as a function of the local authority, are bound by similar statutory duties to health services in relation to their safeguarding children responsibilities (HM Government 2010). Thus an early action is to review the housing needs for the newly-formed family. Only time will tell if the child protection plan has been successful in protecting Jack by monitoring his welfare and providing additional support for his parents.

Markers of good practice: the role of the midwife

Christina recognizes the risk factors for neglect of the unborn baby and helps to ensure a timely and proactive response. She seeks supervision from the named midwife and follows up her telephone referral to children's social care in writing.

Christina is able to play a leading role in the core group who are re-sponsible for ensuring that the requirements of the child protection plan are met.

Although she feels sorry for Trinity, Christina keeps a focus on the need to safeguard and promote the welfare of the child. She is open and honest with the parents as to the reasons for her concerns, informs them of the referral to children's social care and is prepared to offer some flexibility to meet their needs.

Christina ensures that the health visitor has a detailed handover before she discharges the family from her care.

Case 2: Courtney and Kendra – faltering growth

Courtney and Kendra are the 18-month-old twin children of Maxine and Declan, who originate from the Irish travelling community.[5] They are their first-born children. The twins are subject to a child protection plan, under the category of neglect, for a period of nine months, as there have been concerns that they were malnourished and poorly cared for. The initial child protection

---

[5] According to the definition provided by the Department of Education Northern Ireland, the Irish traveller community is 'a community of people ... who are identified (by themselves and others) as people with a shared history, cultures and traditions, including, historically, a nomadic way of life on the island of Ireland. This includes those Travellers who live in "settled" accommodation' (see   www.deni.gov.uk/index/21-pupils-parents-pg/18_pupils_parents-travellers_pg/definition_of_ the__irish_travelling_community_.htm).

conference was followed three months later by a child protection review conference (also known as a CPRC), and a second review conference has been arranged to take place six months after this one. This is in keeping with *Working Together* which sets the parameters for the timing of first and subsequent review conferences (HM Government 2010: 178).

Amanda, the health visitor, is a key member of the core group and has been working closely with Maxine and Declan, children's social care, a family centre worker and a Home-Start volunteer[6] to ensure that the children's needs are met, and that they do not suffer additional harm. She has also been liaising with other health professionals involved with the family, including the GP, community paediatrician and dietician. Amanda arranges for a nursery nurse from the children and family team to provide support and advice on play and activities for the twins. The additional support that has been provided for the family appears to have led to a much improved situation for Courtney and Kendra. Although they remain small, they now appear to be thriving and are reaching their expected developmental milestones. Indeed, with a vocabulary of around 80–100 words and a number of two-word sentences, Kendra appears to be above average in her speech development. Although there were initial difficulties in engaging the parents with the objectives of the child protection plan, they are now appreciating the difference that it has made for the family.

The events that led to the child protection plan began when the children were aged 9 months and concerns were raised via an anonymous call to children's social care that the children were not being fed properly. In the first instance Amanda was asked to make an assessment and to weigh the infants. She had not visited the family since the twins were 3 months old, at which time Declan's mother had been staying and all had appeared to be satisfactory. However, when Amanda called, there was 'no reply' despite the fact that this was an arranged visit. She left a card, and then tried to call, but the mobile telephone number that she had been given previously was unobtainable. A couple of days later Amanda called by on an unannounced visit. This time the door was opened by Declan, who said that the babies were asleep and that it was not convenient to call. He added that it was a bad time for them as he had just lost his job. Given that the initial concerns had been raised by children's social care, Amanda provided an update and a joint visit was arranged.

At this visit the parents were informed that a call had been received concerning the welfare of the children. Both professionals were also concerned to find indications of neglectful care. In respect of the infants' weight, Amanda found that their initial weight gain had tailed off. When plotted on a centile chart, she noted that it had crossed from the 25th to below the third centile, suggesting faltering growth. While it was accepted that the twins were small for their age due to their prematurity and genetic make-up, the current weights, taken in context with other indicators of neglect were a cause of concern (NCCWCH 2009). In addition to the faltering growth, there were other factors of note. These included the fact that Kendra presented with an excoriating nappy rash

---

[6] Home-Start volunteers are trained people with parenting experience who offer emotional and practical help to families. See www.home-start.org.uk/homepage.

and that both infants looked somewhat grubby and pale, with dark shadows under their eyes. When Amanda and the social worker arrived at the house, they were also concerned to find that Courtney was strapped into a buggy, while Kendra was asleep on the sofa. Declan and Maxine had recently become the owners of a puppy, who was in the stages of being 'house-trained'. Both parents presented as 'flat' and somewhat apathetic to the needs of the babies and their new pet. The house was extremely untidy, with piles of damp washing draped over the furniture. Declan explained that his mother had returned to Ireland and that they had not parted in good company, mainly because of the tensions between Maxine and her mother-in-law. The couple also admitted that they had missed an immunization appointment for the twins.

Referral was made via the GP for a paediatric assessment, as it was important to be clear as to the possible cause of the faltering growth. The health visitor also asked the parents to complete a 'food diary' for the twins and arranged a follow-up visit a week later. The key concern was of neglect and that these were unsupported young parents who were struggling with a range of issues, including estrangement from their wider network of family and recent unemployment. There had also been a pattern of neighbour disputes on the new estate where the family were living. Unfortunately, the parents did not comply with the advice to complete the diary, nor did they take the children to the appointment with the paediatrician. As a result of this, Section 47 enquiries were initiated by children's social care, an initial child protection conference was held and the twins were made subject to a child protection plan. The parents attended the conference, and accepted the need for a period of intensive help and monitoring to ensure the well-being of their babies.

Practice question

If you were the health visitor for this family what could you be expected to contribute to the child protection plan?

Faltering growth

Faltering growth is a term that is increasingly used in place of 'failure to thrive' to describe growth patterns in children whereby there is a slowing of growth along the expected trajectories. Although there has been a historical view that child maltreatment is a leading cause of this condition, especially in the absence of disease, more recent studies tend to conclude that this will be the case for only a small minority of cases, with difficulties in feeding being the most common cause (e.g. Batchelor 1999; Underdown 2000; Wright 2005). Health visitors are recognized to be a key source of advice and support for parents who are struggling with infant feeding difficulties, although it is worth noting that the study by Underdown found that conflicting messages from health professionals may be causing additional problems for families.

Practice point

Programmes to address parent-child feeding difficulties draw on the positive parenting techniques that were outlined in Chapter 2 – i.e. parents are encouraged to ignore negative behaviour (food refusal) and to praise positive behaviour (accepting food). This approach can ensure that the tensions surrounding mealtimes are reduced and improvements can be achieved. Support at mealtimes and reviewing videotapes of meals are also helpful (Underdown 2000).

The child protection review conference

There is a constant flux in the numbers and names of children and young people who are subject to a child protection plan, with most plans in place for between 6 and 12 months. The purpose of the child protection review conference is to reconvene a meeting between parents and professionals (children too, where they are of an age to contribute) to review the health and developmental progress of the child/children against the outcomes set out in the child protection plan, amending the plan if necessary. Importantly, it is the point at which an inter-agency decision can be made as to whether or not the plan can be discontinued, and if so, what ongoing support may be needed, including the possibility of a Children Act 1989 Section 17 'child in need' plan being provided.

In order for a child protection plan to be discontinued one of the following must apply:

- the risk of harm has been reduced by the actions of the child protection plan;
- the child and family's circumstances have changed and a plan is no longer needed;
- the child and family have moved permanently to another local authority area (subject to the receiving authority convening a 'transfer-in' conference);
- the child has reached the age of 18 years, has died or permanently left the UK.

Case 2 continued

Kendra and Courtney have been subject to a child protection plan in the category of 'neglect' for nine months. During this period of time there has been an intensive package of multi-agency work with the family. Amanda, the health visitor, plays a key role in ensuring that the children receive their immunizations, attend appointments with the GP, paediatrician and dietician and that these health professionals are aware of the child protection status of the twins. She also plans and supervises the nursery nurse input, which has helped to ensure that Maxine and Declan engage in play activities that support the children's development. Amanda works closely with the allocated social worker to monitor the twins' health and well-being. There are now signs of both improved physical care and pattern of growth. Importantly, the parents have complied with the interventions, and Declan has recently found work. Amanda is anticipating that the outcome of the child protection review conference will be an inter-agency decision to discontinue the child protection plan.

Practice question

If you were the health visitor attending the conference what evidence might you present to persuade colleagues that the children are no longer at risk of significant harm? What would you be able to contribute to the ongoing care to ensure that the children are safeguarded in the future?

This case has provided a 'window' on the processes by which children and young people can be protected from harm and, at a time when safeguarding and child protection have been in the public eye and castigated for 'poor practice', demonstrates that (as happens in the majority of cases) good outcomes can be achieved.

Markers of good practice: the role of the health visitor

Amanda works collaboratively with all those involved in addressing the safeguarding children issues. Her expert knowledge of infant feeding, child health and child development underpins the relationship with other stakeholders, including the parents.

Although children's social care took the statutory lead in managing the child protection aspects, Amanda is a lynchpin in terms of liaising with other health professionals (GP, paediatrician, dietician) and in supporting a nursery nurse in the provision of a programme of play and activities that has been rewarding to both the twins and their parents.

Amanda carefully documents her assessment and produces written reports which she presents at core group and review child protection conferences. These are shared with the parents in advance of these meetings.

In recognizing the intensity of the relationship with this family, and her feelings of distress at the initial visits, Amanda seeks supervision with her allocated supervisor, and additional support from the named nurse safeguarding children.

Amanda completes clear, contemporaneous records of the events and her actions (NMC 2009b).

Case 3: Riley — an accidental ingestion

Riley is an active and inquisitive 4-year-old, who spends alternate weekends with his father, Charlie. The pair have a great deal of fun together and Riley looks forward to the visits. Riley's parents separated when he was 18 months of age. Charlie's substance misuse and addiction was a feature of the ending of their relationship. However, he agreed to attend the local substance misuse service for treatment and being 'clean' is a condition of the courts for his contact time with his son. As part of his treatment, Charlie has been prescribed suboxone (buprenorphine and naloxone), which after an initial requirement to 'consume on premises', he now has dispensed on a weekly basis. This new regime has marked a sustained period of compliance and stability with his treatment.

After a day out at the local zoo, Riley is rather fractious and tired. As a treat, Charlie allows Riley to have a nap in his bedroom. Unfortunately he has failed to remember that his packet of suboxone is on the bedside cabinet. A short while later he finds that Riley has opened the box and that there are a number of tablets missing. Searching frantically he finds one nibbled tablet on the floor, and half a tablet on the bedcover. Riley is difficult to rouse, and is breathing slowly, but noisily. An ambulance is called. Later that day Riley is transferred from the local hospital to the paediatric intensive care unit (PICU) for respiratory support and monitoring. He makes a full recovery.

With support from the hospital's liaison health visitor, PICU staff contact the local children's social care department. A multi-agency strategy discussion, chaired by a senior social worker and involving hospital and community health professionals and the police, is held. While it is accepted that this was an accidental overdose, the need to guard against future risk is clear. The case will progress to a Section 47 enquiry and an initial child protection conference. The local community provider of substance misuse services will also raise the event as a 'serious incident requiring investigation' (SIRI).

The adverse effects of accidental exposure to buprenorphine in young children

A paper by Geib *et al.* (2006) reports on five cases of toddlers with life-threatening respiratory and mental-status depression after accidental ingestion of buprenorphine. This series included children who accessed parental, other relatives' and a family friend's medication. The authors note that sublingual absorption may lead to significant toxicity in small children by merely placing the medication in their mouths. They recommend that parents in homes where buprenorphine is used should be warned of the risks of paediatric exposure.

Case 3 continued

As part of the response to this serious incident, Molly, a substance misuse practitioner, is asked by her manager to work with the local safeguarding children lead to see if there are lessons that can be learned. This request was made under the auspices of the National Patient Safety Agency's (NPSA) *National Framework for Reporting and Learning from Serious Incidents Requiring Investigation* (NPSA 2010). One of the issues raised in the subsequent investigation is the degree to which Charlie's care coordinator considered the implications of the treatment in relation to his contact with Riley (or indeed any other children).

Molly concludes that the way in which the service worked to 'protect' the privacy and confidentiality of their clients, including keeping separate sets of records, led to failures in recording the details of any child care responsibilities, as well as proactive liaison with other agencies. This appears to be contrary to best practice (Cleaver *et al*. 2008).

Molly and her safeguarding lead approach the Local Safeguarding Children Board (LSCB) with a proposal to draw up a protocol to improve joint working. Furthermore, the service's care pathway for the treatment and management of opioid addiction is revised to include more explicit detail of the importance of educating clients and their families about the dangers of accidental ingestion of medication by young children (NICE 2007). Client records are also redesigned to ensure that details of family members, including dependent children, are completed even where they are not members of the same household.

Markers of good practice: the role of the substance misuse practitioner

Molly works jointly with the safeguarding children lead to review this serious incident and consider the learning from it.

Improvements are made to the process of care planning and assessment to ensure that the needs of children (and risks to them) will become an integral part of the care delivered by the service.

Molly seeks to underpin her review with the evidence-base for good practice.

Summary

This chapter has considered neglect as a form of child maltreatment. Neglect is seen as an 'omission' of care that can be deliberate, but more commonly occurs as a result of a range of parental difficulties. The impact of neglect can be as serious as other forms of child maltreatment, including the potential to contribute to the death of a child. Failure to attend for health care is an important indicator of neglect and robust systems need to be in place to ensure that children who are not brought to appointments are followed up. The three cases that have been presented are drawn from the realities of practice. The first case introduced Trinity, Joel and baby Jack. The past history of the parents and their current lifestyle carry a recognized risk of neglect. The second case considered malnutrition and other factors as indicative of the neglect of twins, Courtney and Kendra. A child protection review conference considered whether or not the plan could be discontinued. Finally, a serious incident concerning a young child's accidental ingestion of a prescribed semi-synthetic opioid, with a potentially tragic outcome, was discussed. A community midwife, a health visitor and a substance misuse practitioner were the key professionals involved in the cases. These fictional cases have been portrayed in a realistic way, but the aim here is to demonstrate how easy it can be to 'feel sorry' for the parents. However, the over-arching message, that the daily lived experience of the child is the most important factor in any assessment, is clear.

Key points

- Approximately half of all children and young people who have a child protection plan are categorized as being at risk of neglect.
- An essential theme of neglect is 'omission' or 'absence of care'.
- Neglect can lead to serious outcomes for children and young people, including fatality.
- When children do not attend health appointments this should be conceived as 'was not brought' rather than 'did not attend'.
- Professionals working with neglectful families need to ensure that they access high quality supervision that will both support and challenge their thinking.

7 Child death and serious case review

Learning outcomes

This chapter will help you to:

- Understand the purpose and function of statutory child death review processes (child death overview panel and the rapid response).
- Be aware of the purpose and function of the serious case review.
- Appreciate the role that child death and serious case review processes may play in the prevention of future child deaths and in improvements in practice.
- Gain insight into the role of the designated nurse (and doctor).

Introduction

This chapter aims to help nurses and midwives to gain an appreciation of the inter-agency procedures set out in Chapters 7 and 8 of *Working Together* (HM Government 2010). In this guidance, Chapter 7 outlines the (relatively new) statutory child death review processes for all child deaths in England,[1] while Chapter 8 details the more established process of serious case review for child maltreatment-related deaths and serious child care incidents. Nurses and midwives may be asked to contribute to these reviews, which form an important component of the roles and responsibilities of their named and designated colleagues. Two scenarios are presented to help readers to understand how these processes function and to appreciate the potential wider benefits to the health and safety of all children and young people. As with all the examples in this book, the cases are fictitious, but are drawn from the realities and experiences of practice.

- Case 1 concerns Tegan who has died unexpectedly at the age of 11 weeks. The circumstances of her death, the process of rapid response and the child death review process are outlined.

---

[1] Other countries of the UK have similar processes to those outlined in Chapter 8, and at the time of writing are considering or piloting wider child death review processes.

- Case 2 concerns Preston, aged 7 months, who has sustained a non-accidental head injury. Preston was admitted to a specialist paediatric neurological unit, where he remained very seriously unwell for a number of weeks. A serious case review was requested by the chair of the Local Safeguarding Children Board (LSCB).

The death of an infant, child or young person, whether expected or sudden and unexpected, with or without suspicious circumstances, is a tragedy for all those involved. In the UK today, as in all developed countries, death in childhood is thankfully rare. Because of this, when a child dies there may be a resultant groundswell of action that is concerned with ensuring that lessons are learned or changes made to prevent future child deaths. In many cases such action is led by bereaved family and friends. This would include actions taken to gain meaning and to help to prevent such deaths in the future. Examples here may well include activity following the deaths of children from cancer, road traffic collisions, or the deaths of young people from suicide or self-harm. Child death review processes garner actions of parents, professionals, wider communities and governments to help to learn lessons and make changes to prevent future deaths.

When a child or young person has died or is seriously injured, and abuse or neglect are recognized to have contributed, the circumstances of the case will always be reviewed in some depth to see if lessons can be learned. A minority of child maltreatment deaths will become high profile. In these cases, the public and politicians may also demand action and, caught up with the horror of these deaths, there may be what can only be described as gratuitous vilification of professionals (e.g. in the cases of Victoria Climbié, Peter Connelly and Khyra Ishaq). The effect of this can be devastating, with an ever-present danger that practitioners from the range of agencies who contribute to child protection and safeguarding (i.e. professionals from health, early years, education, children's social care and the police service) will fail to engage in this work, be this at the front line or as a chosen specialty later in their careers. This in turn raises a risk of jeopardizing the safety and well-being of a generation of children, young people and their families. Responses to the death of a child, however caused, must be supportive, proportionate and timely, while maximizing opportunities for improvements in knowledge, professional practice and policies.

In recognizing both the unusualness of death in childhood, as well as the impact of policy on the broader welfare of children, young people and their families, Jenny and Isaac (2006: 265) note that 'The death of a child is a sentinel event in a community, and a defining marker of a society's policies of safety and health'.

Developing an understanding of child death review and serious case review processes aims to assist readers in making the links between preventative action and policies that promote children and young people's safety and health. As such it will help to strengthen and consolidate the learning in child protection and safeguarding that this book aims to promote. The knowledge gained may in turn support nurses and midwives in making practical and positive contributions to improvements in safeguarding and promoting the welfare of children, young people and their families in the future. We begin by outlining the statutory child death review processes.

Child death review processes

Statutory child death review processes became a requirement for LSCBs in England in 2008. These standardized processes and procedures draw on the experiences and learning from other countries (most notably the USA) as well as various 'early starter' panels (Sidebotham *et al.* 2008) and established regional systems in the UK (CEMACH 2008). There are two elements to the statutory requirements:

- the rapid response to unexpected deaths in childhood;
- the child death overview panel.

Not only do these processes seek to offer better support to the families and friends of children who die (especially in helping parents to understand why their child died), they may also serve a valuable public health function in providing information on patterns and causes of child deaths and in informing action to prevent future deaths. Examples of the outcomes of child death review teams in the USA include:

- safe infant sleep campaigns;
- the promotion of the use of smoke detectors (and other home safety equipment);
- legislative changes to enforce and enhance bicycle and vehicle safety;
- immunization campaigns;
- actions to support accessible health care provision to poor and vulnerable families;
- improvements in bereavement services.

In the UK, the largely health-centric review of child deaths in five regions (including Northern Ireland and Wales) has been instrumental in endorsing the benefits of learning from the systematic review of all child deaths. The findings of the report *Why Children Die* (CEMACH 2008) will be of interest to nurses and midwives who work in a variety of settings. The key learning from this review is that:

- death rates of children are higher in families suffering the greatest socio-economic difficulties;
- improvements are needed in accessibility to child and adolescent mental health services (CAMHS), including services for young people affected by substance misuse;
- primary health care workers and emergency departments need to improve their recognition of the sick child;
- there is a need for more health staff to have paediatric or child health training;

- there should be rigorous follow-up of children who miss appointments (see Chapter 6);
- there should be improvements in the palliative and end of life care of children.

The role of the Centre for Maternal and Child Enquiries

The Centre for Maternal and Child Enquiries (CMACE) (previously CEMACH) carries out national confidential enquiries into maternal and child health and a range of other related audit and research activities designed to improve maternal and child health in the UK. National confidential enquiry is a form of national clinical audit and is a method of assessing the quality of care to help identify potentially avoidable factors associated with adverse outcomes. Nurses and midwives may contribute to CMACE activities, and their reports provide good evidence for the best practice in achieving good outcomes for women, infants and children (see www.cmace.org.uk).

Although the majority of child deaths are reported to be 'entirely non-suspicious' (Fox 2008), the child death review process provides an additional opportunity for inter-agency consideration of the possibility of maltreatment as a contributory factor in the death. This function addresses longstanding concerns in the UK and elsewhere that there may be under-ascertainment of such deaths. Equally, there is also the need to respond to public consternation about the incrimination of bereaved parents, particularly in cases where such parents have experienced the unexpected death of more than one of their offspring. Baroness Kennedy's working group on sudden unexpected death in infancy (SUDI) noted that this can only be achieved by building and informing the evidence-base on causation through systematic enquiry (RCP/RCPCH 2004).

Furthermore, while child maltreatment deaths are usually perceived to take place as a result of inflicted physical injury or serious neglect, deaths of children and young people may also occur within the context of historical or longstanding maltreatment, including emotional and sexual abuse. As Jenny and Isaac (2006) add, child maltreatment can be a contributory factor in suicide, as well as deaths arising from young people's risk-taking behaviour that can follow on from earlier abuse or neglect. Child death review processes thus provide opportunities to prevent future child deaths and to impact more widely on the health and well-being of children, young people and their families.

Child death review processes are outlined in Chapter 7 of the statutory guidance (HM Government 2010). The guidance upholds an expectation that all LSCBs in England will ensure that there are procedures in place to support a multi-agency 'rapid response' to unexpected deaths and that all childhood deaths occurring within a local authority area will be reviewed at a child death overview panel (CDOP). The stated purposes of these processes are to identify:

- any cases that may require further investigation, including the need for a serious case review;
- any concern about the health and safety of children in the area;
- any wider public health or safety concerns that arise from a particular death, or pattern of deaths in the area.

The processes are now considered in more detail.

Rapid response

The rapid response to unexpected deaths in childhood is best described as an inter-agency approach that seeks to gather information to help in determining why a child died and to better support the family. The key agencies involved are health and the police, although there is also a role for children's social care and other agencies who may have been involved with the child or their family. NHS Trusts are required to appoint a designated paediatrician for unexpected deaths in childhood who will take an overall lead on rapid response, including offering support and expertise to on-call paediatricians as required. Unexpected deaths in childhood are defined by leading researchers in the field as:
    the death of an infant or child (less than 18 years old) which:

- was not anticipated as a significant possibility, for example, 24 hours before the death; or
- where there was a similarly unexpected collapse leading to or precipitating the events that led to the death.

(HM Government 2010: 212)

> Access your LSCB rapid response protocol so that you are aware of how this system operates in your area. Find out who holds responsibility for the role of designated doctor for unexpected deaths and who takes the role of the senior health care professional in joint home (or place of death) visits.

There are three key phases to the rapid response:

- the immediate response;
- the early response;
- the later response.

The immediate response

The immediate response to a child's unexpected collapse or death will normally involve the transport of the child to an emergency department (ED), with ongoing attempts at resuscitation. Even where it appears as though the child may have been dead for some time, it is considered best practice to take their body to an ED, rather than straight to a mortuary. This will enable any chance of successful resuscitation, help to ensure early expert examination of the child's body by a paediatrician and facilitate the collection of samples and specimens in accordance with legislation[2] and guidance (RCP/RCPCH 2004).

Clearly the ED is also an environment where nursing staff are on hand to offer first-line bereavement support to parents, often in conjunction with a faith leader. Nursing staff who are allocated to care for parents at this time should ensure that the parents are given an opportunity to hold and spend time with their child, while they keep a discreet presence. As noted in *Working Together* in most situations parents are likely to have handled their child in an attempt to resuscitate them and thus allowing them to hold their child will not interfere with the investigation into the cause of death (HM Government 2010). Staff may also offer parents a memento, such as a lock of hair or footprint from their child.

In some cases – for example accidental deaths of older children, or in order to preserve a crime scene – transfer to the ED may not be possible. However, as in all cases of unexpected death in childhood, the key aspects of rapid response, such as inter-agency communication, information sharing and planning, should still occur.

Involvement of the police

The police are involved in all unexpected deaths. Once the death of a child is confirmed a comprehensive health and social history will be gathered jointly by the police and a paediatrician while the family are in the department. This is done primarily to help to ascertain the cause of death and to identify any suspicious indicators. The coroner is also informed of the death, and from this point onwards will have jurisdiction over the body. The paediatrician (either on-call or designated) will initiate an information-sharing and planning meeting between lead agencies (health, police and social care) and others who may have been involved in the care of the child prior to, or around the time of, their death. Contact should be made with other agencies who provided care to the child (e.g. CAMHS, speech and language therapy), both to inform them of the death and to gather any relevant information on the child and family. If child protection or safeguarding issues are raised, it may be necessary to take action to protect surviving siblings.

The joint home visit

A multi-agency decision will also be made at this time as to the appropriateness of a joint home visit (or a visit to the place where the child died) by a police

---

[2] Human Tissue Act 2004.

officer and a senior health care professional. This would normally take place within the first 24 hours following the death and takes the rapid response into the 'early phase'. The health care professional who undertakes the home visit may be a paediatrician, or they may be a specialist nurse who is trained and experienced in unexpected death in childhood. The home visit provides an opportunity to gain additional information about the child, as well as an insight into parenting and environmental factors that may be helpful in determining the reasons for an unexpected child death. Viewing and discussing the sleeping arrangements for the child, including the sleeping surfaces, bedding and any co-sleeping can be particularly helpful. The joint visit also provides an opportunity to support parents and siblings and to provide information to them on other processes, such as the post-mortem examination.

The value of the visit being undertaken by a health professional who is able to benchmark home conditions and provision for the care of children based on extensive experience across diverse populations is self-evident, and is a role that is particularly suited to health visitors. Research undertaken with bereaved parents in areas in which there is an established tradition of joint visits has found that parents reported them to be helpful, rather than intrusive (Fleming *et al*. 2004).

Practice point

Chronic illness, disability and life-limiting conditions will account for a large proportion of deaths in childhood. These children and their families are likely to have had extensive engagement with a range of health care services. Professionals supporting the child and family will need to ensure appropriate support is in place, including end of life care plans, which may state where the child's body is to be cared for after their death (e.g. a cool room at a children's hospice). Although such deaths may be anticipated, they can also be unexpected and should be managed accordingly. As *Working Together* (HM Government 2010: 209) notes: 'This is both out of respect for the child and family, and to fulfil any statutory requirements'.

The early response

Once the preliminary results of the post-mortem are available, a further multi-agency meeting will be convened (or may take place by telephone) to review these, as well as any further information that has come to light, including any safeguarding concerns. Discussions at this point usually involve the pathologist, police, children's social care and the paediatrician, plus other health care professionals, as deemed necessary. This completes the early phase of rapid response.

The later response

The later phase of the rapid response takes place from a week to three to four months after the unexpected death, and is dependent on the full post-mortem report being available. The later response comprises a case discussion involving those who knew the child and family and those involved in investigating the death. The meeting is called and led by the designated paediatrician for unexpected child deaths (or their agreed deputy). Midwives, health visitors and/or school nurses are likely to be invited to contribute to this meeting. The main purpose is to:

- share information to identify the cause of death and/or the factors that may have contributed to it;
- plan for the future care and support of the family;
- highlight potential lessons to be learned;
- inform the inquest;
- decide how, and by whom, information will be shared (including with the parents).

An explicit documented discussion as to the possibility of child maltreatment as a contributory cause of the child's death should be held at this meeting. If there are any suspicious circumstances, then the police will provide guidance on what information from the post-mortem can be shared with the parents by the paediatrician. Reports from this meeting are sent to the coroner. The CDOP also receives a copy of the report, alongside the completed core national data-set documentation (as determined centrally).

The child death overview panel

The CDOP process is the second of the two statutory child death review processes. Like rapid response, it is also described in Chapter 7 of *Working Together* (HM Government 2010). The CDOP, which is made up of senior leads from a range of agencies, is responsible for undertaking a paper-based overview of available information concerning all deaths of children (up to the age of 18 years, excluding stillborn babies and planned lawful terminations) who live within a local authority area (or areas) served by a LSCB. The panel is also responsible for implementing and monitoring the rapid response process.

Practice point

All deaths of children and young people should be notified to the local CDOP co-ordinator. Health professionals should have access to the national forms for making such reports and know how the process operates in their locality. It is important to remember to ensure that children and young people who die at home are notified to the CDOP accordingly.

Local CDOPs usually have a fixed core multi-disciplinary membership drawn from the key agencies who are represented at the LSCB, with others co-opted

Table 7.1 Role and function of CDOP members

Role	Function
Public health consultant	May act as panel chair. Will contribute specialist public health advice on trends, statistics, demography, health protection and prevention
Specialist community public health nurse/ designated nurse safeguarding children	Advice on health care matters (including prevention), child development, specialist safeguarding children knowledge, relevant case information, including bereavement support
Designated paediatrician for child deaths	Advice on pathology, post-mortem results, treatment regimes, relevant case information
Senior manager, children's social care	Advice on child care and safeguarding issues, relevant case information
Senior ambulance officer	Relevant case information and advice on emergency response
Senior manager, education	Advice on education matters, relevant case information
Senior police officer	Advice on criminal and public safety aspects, relevant case information
Co-opted members (e.g. midwife, neonatologist, pathologist, road traffic officer, hospice nurse)	Will attend according to the nature of the deaths being discussed to provide an expert opinion

as necessary (e.g. a road traffic officer if a road traffic collision death is being reviewed). Public health and child health professionals will be core members of the panel. A typical panel and its functions is outlined in Table 7.1.

The functions of the panel include:

- reviewing and evaluating the information on all deaths in the area and identifying issues of concern;
- evaluating specific cases in depth;
- referring any cases that suggest further enquiries, including the need for a serious case review, to the chair of the LSCB;
- considering what can be learned from the death (or patterns of similar deaths in the area);
- providing information to the professionals involved with the child's family;
- monitoring the bereavement support offered to families of children who have died;
- identifying any public health issues and co-operating with regional and national initiatives (e.g. CMACE) to identify lessons on the prevention of child deaths.

Information to support these functions will be sought from those who provided care of the child. Nurses, midwives and health visitors are among those who will be approached to complete an outline of their professional involvement and assessment that may help the panel in its deliberations. A consensus on the degree of preventability of the death is core to the discussion and recommendations of the panel. Such recommendations rest on the identification of 'modifiable' factors. These could be within the family and environment, related to parenting capacity or linked to the provision of services. Crucially, it is the identification of modifiable factors, that are amenable to intervention at a local or national level, that is key to learning lessons and reducing the risk of future child deaths. In terms of reporting to the LSCB, or more widely, each CDOP is expected to produce an annual report that summarizes the numbers and types of deaths reviewed (ensuring anonymity) and outlines any recommendations that are made. As the guidance notes: 'The [CDOP] annual report should serve as a powerful resource for driving public health measures to prevent child deaths and promote child health, safety and wellbeing' (HM Government 2010: 231).

Involvement of parents

My experience, both as a researcher (Sidebotham *et al.* 2008), and in practice, has been that professionals may need clarity and guidance in relation to the involvement of parents and family members in the child death review processes. The Foundation for the Study of Infant Deaths (FSID) has produced an excellent leaflet called *Child Death Review: A Guide for Parents and Carers* (FSID 2010) that can be ordered as a hard copy or downloaded from the website.[3] This leaflet, which should be made readily available to all bereaved parents, also serves as a useful introduction to child death review for health professionals.

In essence, when a child dies, the parents should be informed that their child's death will be reviewed by a CDOP. Where the death of a child is unexpected, the rapid response process has a number of points of direct contact with families, and there is anecdotal and research-based evidence that parents find this helpful. Parents should be assured that the key objective of the CDOP is to learn lessons that may help to improve the health, safety and well-being of children and to prevent future deaths. Although it is not appropriate for parents to attend panel meetings, they should be encouraged to contribute any comments or questions they might have to the review and the panel will need to ensure that feedback is provided accordingly. As noted at the outset, taking action and learning lessons from the tragedy of child death may help parents, families, professionals and communities to address the terrible loss of a child and find some meaning in being able to better protect the health, safety and well-being of others.

---

[3] See http://fsid.org.uk.

Case 1: Tegan — an unexpected death in infancy

Following a restless and difficult day, Tegan, who is 11 weeks old, falls asleep cuddled up with her mother Carys on the sofa. When Carys awakes at around 3 a.m. she realizes that Tegan is cold and pale. An ambulance is called and mother and baby are taken to the ED at the local general hospital. Sadly, Tegan is declared dead some 40 minutes later.

Sudden unexpected death in infancy

SUDI is reported to be far less common than in the past and this has been related to changes made as a result of increased understanding of factors that may contribute to such deaths (RCP/RCPCH 2004). An FSID fact-file for parents and carers that summarizes the most recent research into the prevention of SUDI makes a number of recommendations. A key theme relates to the prime importance of ensuring a safe sleeping environment, with the over-arching message being 'The safest place for your baby to sleep is on their back in a crib or cot in a room with you for the first six months'.

Some SUDIs will be labelled as sudden infant death syndrome (SIDS), which is essentially a diagnosis of exclusion. The leading non-SIDS causes have been noted to be infection, cardiovascular anomaly, child abuse and metabolic or genetic disorder (Loughrey *et al.* 2005). Parents will have 'mounting and reasonable' expectations that the cause of the death of their infant will be identified and it is thus important that any SUDI is thoroughly investigated (RCP/RCPCH 2004). Rapid response will assist with this.

Case 1 continued

Mei, a named nurse for safeguarding children, has undertaken additional training to enable her to make a key contribution to the local rapid response process. Following the immediate care of the family and infant in the ED and a multi-agency strategy discussion, Mei undertakes a joint home visit with a non-uniformed police officer from the local child abuse investigation unit.

At the home visit Mei is able to offer bereavement support to Tegan's family and make an assessment of the home conditions, in particular the infant care and sleeping arrangements. She notes that the flat is very warm and that there is a smell of stale tobacco smoke. Mei also gathers information from the health visitor who had undertaken an ante-natal visit and new birth visit. Reports of the home visit are shared at the second strategy meeting at which a preliminary finding of cause of death from the post-mortem examination is reported as 'positional asphyxia'. No further significant information is raised at the final strategy meeting which meets to review the case and to consider ongoing support to the family, as well as issues that will be reported to the local CDOP.

Table 7.2 Information for a CDOP

Child	Family and environment
Normal delivery at 36 weeks gestation	Few details known about father
Healthy small infant, birth weight 2.43 kg	Mother not in a relationship
First child of young mother	Mother smoked 6–10 cigarettes per day
Initially breast-fed, but formula since 3 weeks of age	during pregnancy, says to have reduced and smokes outside
Slow to gain weight, last recorded weight 3.56 kg	Drinks 1–2 units of alcohol daily (cider)
Smiled at 7 weeks of age	Privately rented flat
Noted to have had a mild nappy rash at visit to child health clinic, otherwise has appeared well cared for	Heating kept turned up due to tendency for dampness
	On benefits
Not yet had first immunization	Last worked as a retail assistant pre-pregnancy
	Own mother lives locally
	Few friends

Parenting capacity	Services provided
Enjoyed pregnancy and attended for all ante-natal care	Shared care arrangements with maternity department and GP
Some support from own mother, but found role as single parent tiring	Assessed as low risk at new birth contact and invited to attend child health clinic at local children's centre
Warm and loving relationship with Tegan	
SIDS prevention discussed (including safe sleep)	Not seen by HV ante-natally due to staff shortages caused by recruitment difficulties

The CDOP notes Tegan's death as part of its responsibility to undertake an overview of all deaths in the area. The panel also decides to review the case in more depth at a future meeting. This means that further information will be gathered from each agency so that factors in the child, family and environment, parenting capacity and service provision can be more fully discussed and recommendations made. Table 7.2 highlights the type of information that may be provided by the health visitor on the family and the child.

Learning from the child death overview panel process

The case of Tegan demonstrates how child death review processes can be used to support bereavement care and learning to prevent future deaths. Nurses and midwives have a major role to play in contributing at a number of levels. Because there have been several SUDIs in the local authority area, the LSCB decide to launch a 'Safe Sleep' campaign based on the CDOP recommendations. This is led by a midwife and a police officer. Following the campaign there is a drop in the number of SUDIs reported locally and the campaign is shared more widely across the region.

At any point before or during the rapid response or child death overview panel processes, concerns may arise as to the possibility of child maltreatment as a contributory factor in the death of a child or young person. In these instances Chapter 8 processes (HM Government 2010) will be instigated, and may lead to the completion of a serious case review.

Serious case review

In contrast with child death review processes, the serious case review process has been established for some time in England, Wales and Northern Ireland, although it has been introduced more recently in Scotland (Vincent 2009). According to the guidance, the prime purpose of a serious case review is to learn lessons from serious child care incidents and child maltreatment deaths and to improve the safeguarding children practice of individuals and agencies (HM Government 2010). The daily lived experience of the child is seen to be central to maximizing the learning from such events. Importantly, a serious case review is not an investigation into how a child died, or who was responsible. These are issues that the coroner and criminal courts will determine. Serious case reviews are also not part of any disciplinary enquiry into an individual's practice; this would be a matter for the employing organization. In essence, serious case reviews aim to improve inter-agency working to safeguard and promote the welfare of children, albeit that the learning is based on the tiny minority of cases that are at the severe end of the spectrum of child maltreatment, and centres on the notion of failure, rather than success in child protection practice.

As detailed in the guidance, LSCBs will always conduct a serious case review when a child dies (including by suspected suicide) and abuse or neglect are known or suspected to be a factor. This may include situations where a child has been killed by a mentally ill parent or carer, or where substance misuse or domestic violence are known to be present. LSCBs may also commission a serious case review when a child has been seriously harmed and it is thought that there may be lessons to be learned about the way in which local services worked together. This would include cases involving children who have received life-threatening injuries or permanent impairment, or following serious sexual abuse, or when a parent has been murdered or where a child has been harmed following a serious assault perpetrated by another child or an adult (see HM Government 2010 for more details as to when a review is indicated). Some, but by no means all, cases will already be known to children's social care or other targeted or specialist services and a minority may have been subject to a child protection plan. Given the universality of health care services, it would be extremely unusual if the case was not known to health professionals. This means that health services (and for school-age children, education services) are key contributors to serious case reviews.

Practice point

In cases that may progress to a serious case review (or other processes outlined in Chapter 8) practitioners will be asked to hand their records to their safeguarding lead. This is known as 'securing records' and its purpose is to guard against loss or interference and to allow the organization to begin to draw up chronologies of its involvement with the child and family. It does not indicate mistrust of front-line practitioners.

LSCBs normally have a multi-agency serious case review sub-committee which aids the decision-making of the LSCB chair as to whether or not a serious case review should be undertaken. This sub-committee will also oversee and quality assure the reviews. This includes monitoring the achievement of the 'action plan'. Health services are represented on this committee through their commissioning organization. In most cases the representative will be the designated nurse and/or designated doctor for safeguarding children.

Serious case reviews should normally be completed in a set timescale (currently six months) and their format is guided by terms of reference negotiated by the LSCB chair and serious case review sub-committee. The terms of reference, drawn up at the outset, will consider the following:

- How to ensure that key issues (e.g. mental health of parents or carers) are obtained and analysed.
- Setting the dates for the period of time to be reviewed – i.e. how far back? (This will form the basis of the chronology described below.)
- What background factors might help to understand the situation.
- How the child (where the review does not involve a death), surviving siblings, parents or other family members may be supported to contribute to the review.
- How ethnicity, religion, diversity or equality issues should be considered.
- Details about the family's immigration status.
- Who should contribute reports to the serious case review.
- Who should author the overview report and chair the SCR panel.
- How the review sits with other processes (e.g. criminal/coronial proceedings, homicide/suicide reviews, NHS serious incidents requiring investigations (SIRIs).
- How the review can take account of lessons from research, including biennial reviews (e.g. Brandon et al. 2009).
- How family, public and media interest may be managed.

The components of a serious case review

The panel below summarizes the components of, and terminology relating to serious case reviews, with a focus on the contribution of named and designated professionals. It includes details of the process of internal management reviews undertaken by each contributing agency, the overview report and the executive summary. Experience suggests that it is normally nurses who author health internal management reviews,[4] and that in doing so they will look to their managers to ensure that they have the opportunity to attend briefings and undertake training for this role and are freed up from other duties for the time-consuming process of producing their report. LSCB procedures will normally have a chapter on the expectations for the format of reports in their area. These do vary, but in essence there is an expectation that they will be compliant with the statutory guidance (HM Government 2010).

The serious case review process

Serious case review sub-committee

This is normally a standing LSCB sub-committee that oversees and quality assures serious case reviews from commission to completion of action plans arising from recommendations for individual agencies and LSCBs. Minimum membership comprises representatives from local authority children's social care, health (commissioning Primary Care Trust and other partners as relevant), education and the police service.

Serious case review panel

The serious case review panel is commissioned by the serious case review sub-committee to manage and coordinate the process. Members are drawn from the agencies that are represented on serious case review sub-committees, although an independent person (who is not a member of the LSCB involved in the serious case review or an employee of any of the agencies involved) will be appointed to chair the panel.

Chronology

Templates for the completion of agencies' chronologies should be provided within LSCB procedures and/or at the outset of a serious case review. It is important that all agencies use the same template because chronologies will need to be amalgamated. Chronologies are basically a summary of contact with the child and family over a predetermined period of time leading to the death or serious injury. Headings may include the following: date and time; source (e.g. health visitor record); and significant information from the contact, including whether the child was seen, and their wishes and feelings sought and recorded. A final column usually invites comments from the internal management review author. Chronologies can be very powerful tools and may be used in circumstances other than a serious

---

[4]Nurses generally have more time built into their job roles to undertake named and designated duties when compared with medics. Many named and designated nurses now hold these roles on a full-time basis.

case review, for example in cases of fabricated or induced illness (FII) – see Chapter 3.

Internal management review

Drawing on the information provided in the notes, chronology and interviews with involved practitioners, each agency will produce an internal management review. The aim of this review is to 'look openly and critically at individual and organisational practice and the context in which people were working to see . . . if improvements could and should be made' (HM Government 2010: 244). Within health agencies, internal management reviews are normally authored by named professionals (nurses), with lead GPs increasingly taking responsibility to author these reviews concerning the child and family's contact with general practice. Details of the scope and format of these reviews can be found on pages 245–6 of the statutory guidance. Authors should not have had clinical involvement with the family.

Health overview report

Designated safeguarding children professionals (usually the nurse) act on behalf of the Trust as commissioners and are responsible for reviewing and evaluating the practice of all involved health professionals in the Trust area (including GPs). Designated professionals are responsible for producing an integrated health chronology and 'an objective, just and thorough' health overview report that focuses on how health organizations have worked together (HM Government 2010: 243). If designated professionals have been clinically involved in the case they should seek help from another Trust-designated professional.

Overview report

An independent overview report author will bring together the information from the constituent reviews and chronologies. This will include an anonymized genogram (a family tree) showing the relationship of the family, extended family and household. The information should be analysed in some depth to consider, with the benefit of hindsight, if different decisions or actions may have led to a different outcome. Good practice should also be highlighted and the report should be both objective and underpinned by messages from research. The serious case reviews panel is responsible for ensuring that the report is of a high standard.

Action plans

Action plans are drawn up by each agency contributing an internal management review, and, in addition, the serious case review panel will develop an LSCB action plan that arises from recommendations from the overview report. An action plan will need to be formally acknowledged by senior managers from contributing organizations and robust arrangements made to ensure timely implementation and monitoring of the actions.

Executive summary

Although anonymized overview reports are now published in full, the executive summary, which comprises a summary of the circumstances and events, key themes arising from the case, priorities for learning and change, and the recommendations and action plan(s), is a useful tool for learning.

Ofsted grading

Ofsted (Office for Standards in Education) provides quality assurance on internal management reviews and serious case reviews and awards grades accordingly. There are four grades ranging from inadequate to outstanding. Ofsted also publishes periodic reports that provide an overview of lessons from the reviews and a summary of the grades awarded.

Publication of serious case review overview reports

Serious case reviews have been in the public eye during the course of the preparation of material for this book. Following pressure that reflected the public and political milieu in the Peter Connelly case, the Department for Education (DfE) published a letter outlining changes to statutory guidance that mean that serious case reviews overview reports, as well as executive summaries, must be published in full (DfE 2010a). In the letter it is argued that publication was in the greater public interest noting:

> We recognise that the publication of Serious Case Reviews [SCRs] is a sensitive and complex matter. Serious Case Review overview reports contain personal information and it is vitally important that published Serious Case Reviews are appropriately redacted and anonymised to protect the privacy and welfare of vulnerable children and families. There is an important balance to be struck between transparency and openness so that lessons can be learned, and the protection and welfare of individuals.

Shortly after this letter was circulated, the DfE published Haringey LSCB's overview report into the Peter Connelly case, having removed details that might identify his siblings and parents (DfE 2010b).

Recent research into learning lessons from serious case reviews reflects the importance of ensuring that practitioners who find themselves drawn into the process are adequately supported and provided with feedback in terms of lessons learned (Sidebotham *et al.* 2010). While those who took part in the study agreed that serious case reviews were not about apportioning blame, it was noted that this should not detract from ensuring accountability for practice. Contributing to, or indeed authoring a serious case review, can be a stressful experience and it is important that feedback and the opportunity to de-brief are offered.

The following brief case scenario considers the serious case review process in action.

Case 2: Preston — non-accidental head injury leading to permanent disability

Preston, aged 7 months, is admitted to a specialist paediatric neurological unit having sustained a non-accidental head injury (NAHI). At the time of the injury he was in the care of his mother Trudie, and her new boyfriend Derek. Preston is presented to the ED by his distraught mother following a 'fit', having been irritable and unwell for the previous 24 hours. Other significant features noted at the time of his admission to hospital include retinal haemorrhages, small bruises to the upper arms and a left posterior rib fracture. He is also somewhat grubby and underweight. There are signs of an 'old' healing fracture of the femur. Neither adult admits causing the injuries to Preston and because of this police are unable to progress criminal charges. However, the local authority children's social care department follows initial child protection proceedings with care proceedings and Preston is placed with foster carers. As a result of his injuries Preston will live with multiple disabilities, including cerebral palsy and blindness. He is not expected to survive his childhood.

Non-accidental head injury

Non-accidental (or inflicted) head injury is said to be the leading cause of death from physical child abuse, with an incidence of 1 in 3,000 babies under the age of 6 months. The primary cause is shaking, or shaking and impact, or impact only. The most common type of brain injury is a subdural haemorrhage, with or without a subarachnoid haemorrhage. Babies presenting with suspected NAHI will undergo a full examination, including specialist scans and skeletal surveys. Metabolic or haematological conditions will need to be excluded. For those children who do not die from their injuries there may be significant long-term disabilities, learning and behavioural problems (WCPSRG/NSPCC 2009b).

Case 2 continued

The decision to commission a serious case review is based on the severity of Preston's injuries and the fact that his family are known to a range of services. Preston is not subject to a child protection plan. Preston's mother, who is 16 years of age and a care-leaver, has been known to engage in substance misuse in the past. Although there has been some contact with children's social care, that organization was unaware of the arrival of Derek in the household. Derek is known to police for criminal damage and theft and the police have also been called to his previous home following reports of domestic abuse, which at the time was said to be 'verbal only'. Preston was also seen at the local 'walk-in' centre one month prior to his head injury with reports that he was not moving his leg. Reassurance was given by the nurse practitioner who examined him, as it was not apparent that he was in any pain, and there were no visible injuries.

Practice point

Physical abuse is rarely a single event and many infants who suffer NAHI will have had previous episodes of abuse (WCPSRG/NSPCC 2009b).

Elizabeth, the designated nurse for safeguarding children at the local Primary Care Trust will be writing the health overview report. This is to be based on independent management reviews from the lead GP, the hospital named nurse, the community provider named nurse, the safeguarding lead from mental health services (in relation to contact with young people's substance misuse services) and the named midwife. Others contributing internal management reviews will include the local authority children's social care department, the housing association and the police. The independent chair will meet with Trudie and her mother to invite their contributions and to keep them informed of progress.

Although agencies have not yet completed their reports, a pattern of potential missed opportunities to protect Preston from harm is emerging. Most notably for health services there are concerns about:

- the quality of the handover from the midwife to the health visitor;
- the lack of information-sharing between substance misuse services and midwifery;
- the quality of record-keeping;
- the poor quality of assessment of an apparent injury to a non-mobile child at the walk-in centre;
- the GP's failure to consider the needs of the child when Trudie consulted her following a domestic abuse incident;
- a lack of supervision and support to the health visiting team who were clearly struggling to manage the needs of a very large caseload within a deprived population.

Elizabeth is considering making recommendations in relation to improvements in single and inter-agency training, communication and information-sharing, clinical supervision and support, the appointment of practitioners with paediatric expertise at the walk-in centre and record-keeping practice. In addition to the monitoring arrangements at the LSCB serious case review committee, the Trust will ensure that action plans are brought to the clinical governance committees.

Although the format of action plans varies according to LSCB procedures, a typical plan will include the information shown in Table 7.3.

Implementation of actions arising from serious case reviews can take up to two years, depending on their complexity and the capacity of individuals and agencies to make changes. In my experience it is important to be realistic and also to limit single agency recommendations to between four and six proposals.

Preston will not return to his mother's care. He will be cared for in a specialist foster setting, with additional input from a range of professionals, including a community children's nurse. Should Trudie enter another relationship and become pregnant, an early discussion will need to take place between children's social care, the police and midwifery services to plan for the future safety of the unborn child.

Summary

The chapter began by outlining the 'Chapter 7' child death review processes: rapid response and child death overview panel. The first of these processes concerns a phased inter-agency approach to responding to unexpected deaths in childhood, while the second concerns the overview of all child deaths within an area. These are statutory processes that are defined by the systematic collection and sharing of data, driven by the need to prevent future child deaths and designed to better support families whose children have died. The case of Tegan illustrated the rapid response and the CDOP in action, and a campaign for promoting safe sleeping of infants was launched as a result of this work.

The chapter went on to outline the 'Chapter 8' processes of serious case review. This included consideration of the process by which serious case reviews are commissioned, as well as the component parts of chronology, independent management review, overview report and executive summary. These well established statutory processes are primarily concerned with learning lessons from serious child care incidents and child maltreatment deaths which aim to improve the safeguarding children practice of individuals and agencies. Families are invited to contribute to serious case reviews and need to be supported accordingly. Named and designated professionals, especially nurses holding these titles, play an important role in the process. Nurses and midwives who provide care to children, young people and their families may find themselves contributing and need to be supported and de-briefed accordingly. In the case of Preston, who suffered irreversible damage as a result of a NAHI, the

Table 7.3 Serious case review: action plan

No.	Recommendations	Action	Evidence	Outcome	Lead officer	Date for completion	Progress (RAG)
1	These will reflect the recommendations outlined in the report	Action needed to achieve the recommendations Needs to be: SMART **S**pecific **M**easureable **A**chievable **R**ealistic **T**imely	How will you provide assurance that the action has been completed? For example, a new policy or copies of meeting notes	How this action will improve services to children and families and better safeguard and protect children	Name or designation of person responsible	For example, six months after publication of the report	This column will be used to monitor progress on an agreed 'RAG' (i.e. red, amber, green) rating

designated nurse began to pull together the health overview report and consider the learning from this tragic case.

Most importantly, enacting recommendations for practice improvement can be a positive force arising from child maltreatment tragedies.

Key points

- Child death review processes provide opportunities to prevent future child deaths and to impact more widely on the health and well-being of children, young people and their families.
- Death rates of children are higher within families suffering the greatest socioeconomic difficulties.
- The child death review process provides an additional opportunity for inter-agency consideration of the possibility of maltreatment as a contributory factor.
- The prime purpose of a serious case review is to learn lessons from serious child care incidents and child maltreatment deaths and to improve the safeguarding children practice of individuals and agencies.
- Contributing to a serious case review can be a stressful experience and it is important that feedback and the opportunity to de-brief are offered.
- Recommendations for practice improvement can be a positive force arising from child maltreatment tragedies.

8 Messages for practice

Learning outcomes

This final chapter will help you to:

- Embed your learning about safeguarding and child protection in practice.
- Maximize your potential to make a difference to the outcomes of children, young people and their families.
- Promote the importance of the unique contribution of nurses, midwives and health visitors to the safeguarding and child protection processes.
- Practise with enhanced confidence.

Introduction

This practical text has aimed to develop the safeguarding and child protection knowledge, skills and competence of the nursing and midwifery workforce in order that a perceived potential to make an important and unique contribution to the field is realized. The intention has been to reflect the full spectrum of safeguarding children work, from prevention and early intervention through to the contribution to serious case review, and to give examples of different types of child maltreatment, reflecting the input of a range of nursing and midwifery practitioners in acute and community settings. The basis for learning has been the case scenarios, in which the aim has been to highlight good practice. The text has been supported by reference to the evidence base – much of the policy, legislation and guidance is easily accessible via the internet and readers may like to develop their knowledge further through perusal of key texts.

This final chapter provides an opportunity to reinforce learning. However, it is also suggested that the best practice learning is experiential and readers are encouraged to seek opportunities to develop their knowledge, skills and competence. An approach can be made to safeguarding leads – i.e. named and designated professionals – who will be delighted to arrange shadowing activities and to share learning from local cases. I hope that we can give birth to a new generation of nursing and midwifery safeguarding leads!

Key learning points

- Safeguarding children applies to individuals from pre-birth to 18 years of age.
- Children's rights and child-centredness are essential to the delivery of safe, effective care and the achievement of best outcomes.
- Parents have the overriding responsibility to ensure that their children are safe.
- Child maltreatment is a major contemporary public health issue, but it is also open to a public health solution.
- Nurses and midwives who see children in the course of their practice should be familiar with child care and development and have a sound understanding of indicators of possible child maltreatment.
- One in 10 children experience child abuse or neglect in the course of their childhood.
- Adult mental health problems, substance misuse and domestic violence are significant risk factors for child maltreatment.
- Children who are disabled have a three-fold risk of being abused, but are under-represented in safeguarding systems.
- Sensitivity to race, culture and ethnicity is important, however, child abuse cannot be condoned for religious or cultural reasons.
- Confidentiality in a patient−client relationship is not absolute; this should be explained to clients at the outset of any therapeutic relationship.
- Those providing contraception and sexual health services need to practise within the framework of legislation and guidance.
- When children do not attend health appointments this should be viewed as 'was not brought' rather than 'did not attend'.
- Death rates of children are higher within families suffering the greatest socioeconomic difficulties.
- Child death review processes provide opportunities to prevent future child deaths and to impact more widely on the health and well-being of children, young people and their families.
- The prime purpose of a serious case review is to learn lessons from serious child care incidents and child maltreatment deaths and to improve the safeguarding children practice of individuals and agencies.
- Recommendations for practice improvement can be a positive force arising from child maltreatment tragedies.
- Clear, contemporaneous records of events and actions should be kept; good record-keeping is essential in safeguarding and child protection.
- Support and advice on any aspect of safeguarding children can be obtained from named and designated professionals.

Safeguarding and child protection quiz

1 Who are the lead statutory agencies for safeguarding children?
2 What are the seven golden rules of information-sharing?
3 What is positive parenting?
4 What are the three domains for assessment of children in need/ Common Assessment Framework (CAF)?
5 What are the benefits of the Family Nurse Partnership (FNP) programme?
6 What is the most common sign of physical abuse?
7 Why is bruising in a non-mobile child of concern?
8 What features would lead you to suspect non-accidental thermal injury?
9 What is fabricated and induced illness (FII) and how may this present?
10 What is the timescale for following up a telephone referral to children's social care?
11 What is tier-two child and adolescent mental health services (CAMHS)?
12 What happens at a strategy discussion?
13 How may young people be groomed for sexual exploitation?
14 What is the most common category for children and young people made subject to a child protection plan?
15 What is another term for 'failure to thrive'?
16 What is the purpose of the core group?
17 How often should a child protection plan be reviewed and where does this happen?
18 What is the purpose of a chronology?
19 What is a genogram?
20 What are the benefits of clinical supervision in safeguarding children?
21 What are the steps of the rapid response to unexpected deaths in childhood?
22 What is the purpose of the child death overview panel (CDOP)?
23 What is an internal management review?
24 How can learning from serious case review improve practice?

Support for practice: are the following in place for you?

	Tick
I have access to my organization's safeguarding children policy and procedures	
I have access to my Local Safeguarding Children Board (LSCB) policy and procedures	
I know how to contact my named and designated professionals	
I know how to contact my local children's social care department	
I have regular clinical/child protection supervision	
I update my safeguarding and child protection knowledge in accordance with my organization's programme of statutory and mandatory training	

Conclusion

The importance of safeguarding and child protection being 'everyone's responsibility' has been promoted throughout this book. This includes all branches of the nursing and midwifery professions. At the time of writing, there are reported to be more than 665,000 nurses and midwives on the professional register (NMC 2010). Given the 'reach' of this workforce into families and communities, there is much that can be achieved by simply adhering to, and learning from, the basics of good safeguarding children practice outlined in this book. The keys to success is informed, authoritative practice that keeps a focus firmly on the child, a low threshold for concerns and high expectations of parents and service delivery. Taking such a stance provides us with the best opportunity to ensure that no more child protection 'scandals' bring shame and sorrow to families, communities, health professionals, the wider children's workforce and society as a whole. The children, young people and families introduced throughout this book are, of course, not 'real', but their situations are very much so. The sign of the learning from this book will be reflected in the professional response of readers who meet families like these tomorrow.

Appendix

Safeguarding and child protection policy in England

The statutory guidance for England (HM Government 2010) outlines expectations that 'all agencies and professionals' will be alert to potential indicators of maltreatment and the risks that abusers may pose to children; that they will share and analyse information to inform assessments of harm; that they will make a contribution to safeguarding and promoting the child's welfare; that they will take part in reviews against specific plans and work cooperatively with parents (unless this would place the child at greater risk). Most importantly, the guidance recognizes the need to focus on the child, in stating that professionals should 'prioritise direct communication and positive and respectful relationships with children, ensuring the child's wishes and feelings underpin assessments and any safeguarding activities' (HM Government 2010: 32).

Health bodies are named alongside other statutory agencies in having a duty under Section 11 of the Children Act 2004 to ensure that 'their functions are discharged with regard to the need to safeguard and promote the welfare of children' (p. 40). This applies to all those working in the health sector, whether in the NHS or the independent sector, and it is notable that provision for safeguarding children is a key aspect of regulatory expectations and inspection.[1]

Safeguarding and child protection policy in Wales

The Welsh Assembly Government (WAG) takes the lead for policy for children and young people in Wales. Drawing on the United Nations Convention on the Rights of the Child (1989), and in consultation with children, young people and their families, the WAG has developed its 'seven core aims' which state that:

- every child should have a flying start in life and the best possible basis for their future growth and development;
- every child and young person has access to a comprehensive range of education, training and learning opportunities, including the acquisition of essential personal and social skills;

---

[1]The Care Quality Commission (CQC) regulates health and social care provision and this includes review of arrangements for safeguarding children and young people – see www.cqc.org.uk.

- every child and young person enjoys the best possible physical and mental, social and emotional health, including freedom from abuse, victimization and exploitation;
- all children and young people have access to play, leisure, sporting and cultural activities;
- all children and young people are listened to, treated with respect and have their race and cultural identity recognized;
- all children and young people should have a safe home and community which supports physical and emotional well-being;
- no child or young person is disadvantaged by poverty.[2]

Safeguarding children policy and practice is primarily linked to the sixth core aim, 'safe home and community'. The WAG has also published a version of *Working Together* as the principality's statutory guidance (WAG 2007). This document outlines the roles and responsibilities of those working and volunteering with children, young people and their families in Wales. In addition to the statutory guidance, an alliance of organizations for children known as 'Children in Wales'[3] (which includes representatives from all Welsh Safeguarding Children Boards) has produced guidance known as the *All Wales Child Protection Procedures* (All Wales Child Protection Procedures Review Group 2008). Nurses and midwives in Wales should ensure that they have access to this document to support their safeguarding children practice. The *All Wales Child Protection Procedures* are available from the Children in Wales website.

Safeguarding and child protection policy in Scotland

In Scotland safeguarding children and young people work is the responsibility of the Scottish government.[4] Here the policy is underpinned by a *Framework for Standards* (Scottish Executive 2004) and is linked to the Scottish government's 'safer and stronger' objectives for local communities. As with the policy of other countries, there are explicit links to the United Nations Convention on the Rights of the Child (1989) and the protective rights for children. The framework builds on extensive consultation with children and young people and explicitly promotes messages for children who may be being abused or neglected. It states that those who are concerned that they are at risk of harm, or are being harmed, can expect to:

- get the help you need when you need it;
- be seen by a professional such as a teacher, doctor or social worker to make sure you are alright and not put at more risk;
- be listened to seriously, and professionals will use their power to help you;
- be able to discuss issues in private when, and if, you want to;

---

[2]See http://wales.gov.uk/topics/childrenyoungpeople/?lang=en.
[3]See www.awcpp.org.uk/areasofwork/safeguardingchildren/awcpprg/proceduresandprotocols/index.html.
[4]See www.scotland.gov.uk/Topics/People/Young-People/children-families/17834.

- be involved with, and helped to understand, decisions made about your life; and
- have a named person to help you.

(Scottish Executive 2004)

Safeguarding and child protection policy in Northern Ireland

Northern Ireland, in common with the rest of the UK, has developed a strategic outcomes-based framework to support policy to improve the lives, and life chances, of children (Office of the First Minister and Deputy First Minister Northern Ireland 2006). This document states a commitment to ensure that by the year 2016 there will be evidence that children and young people are:

- Healthy;
- Enjoying, learning and achieving;
- Living in safety and with stability;
- Experiencing economic and environmental well-being;
- Contributing positively to community and society; and
- Living in a society which respects their rights.

(Office of the First Minister and Deputy First Minister
Northern Ireland 2006: 7)

In 2009, with support from the National Society for the Prevention of Cruelty to Children (NSPCC), the government issued a cross-departmental policy statement on safeguarding children and child protection. The purpose of this document was to take forward and develop the 'living in safety and with stability' commitment of the 10-year strategy. The document adopted the broader notion of safeguarding, which is defined as incorporating 'all preventable harm that impacts on the lives of children, with a clear focus on children's personal development and well being, and making children's lives better' (Office of the First Minister and Deputy First Minister Northern Ireland 2009: 6).

At the time of writing many of the policy statements' proposals to improve safeguarding children in Northern Ireland were in progress. In particular a redrafting of the statutory guidance *Co-operating to Safeguard Children* (DHSSPS 2003) was underway, as were proposals to give a statutory footing to a newly established independent Safeguarding Board Northern Ireland.

References

ACMD (Advisory Council on the Misuse of Drugs) (2003) *Hidden Harm: Responding to the Needs of Children of Problem Drug Users*. London: Home Office/ACMD.

All Wales Child Protection Procedures Review Group (2008) *All Wales Child Protection Procedures*, www.awcpp.org.uk/areasofwork/safeguardingchildren/awcpprg/procedures andprotocols/index.html, accessed 5 April 2010.

Association of Paediatric Emergency Medicine, British Association of Emergency Medicine, British Association of Paediatric Surgeons, College of Emergency Medicine, Joint Royal Colleges Ambulance Liaison Committee, Royal College of General Practitioners, Royal College of Nursing, Royal College of Paediatrics and Child Health (2007) *Services for Children in Emergency Departments: Report of the Intercollegiate Committee for Services for Children in Emergency Departments*. London: RCPCH.

Audit Commission (2010) *Giving Children a Healthy Start: Health Report February 2010*. London: Audit Commission.

Barlow, J. and Schrader-Macmillan, A. (2009) *Safeguarding Children from Emotional Abuse – What Works?* London: DfES.

Barnes, J., Ball, M., Meadows, P., Belsky, J. and the FNP Implementation Research Team (2009) *Nurse-Family Partnership Programme Second Year Pilot Sites Implementation in England: The Infancy Period*. London: Institute for the Study of Children, Families and Social Issues, Birkbeck, University of London.

Batchelor, J. (1999) *Failure to Thrive in Young Children: Research and Practice Evaluated*. London: The Children's Society.

Benger, J. and McCabe, S. (2001) Burns and scalds in pre-school children attending accident and emergency: accident or abuse? *Emergency Medicine Journal*, 18: 172–4.

Birmingham Safeguarding Children Board (2010) *Serious Case Review Under Chapter VIII 'Working Together to Safeguard Children' in Respect of the Death of a Child, Case Number 14*. Birmingham: Birmingham Safeguarding Children Board.

Brandon, M., Bailey, S., Belderson, P. *et al.* (2008) *Analysing Child Deaths and Serious Injuries through Abuse and Neglect: What Can We Learn? A Biennial Analysis of Serious Case Reviews 2003–2005*. London: DCSF.

Brandon, M., Bailey, S., Belderson, P. *et al.* (2009) *Understanding Serious Case Reviews and their Impact: A Biennial Analysis of Serious Case Reviews 2005–2007*. London: DCSF.

Brown, D.W., Anda, R.F., Tiemeier H. *et al.* (2009) Adverse childhood experiences and the risk of premature mortality, *American Journal of Preventative Medicine*, 37(5): 389–96.

Burton, S. (2009) The oversight and review of cases in the light of changing circumstances and new information: how do people respond to new (and challenging) information? *Safeguarding Children Briefing 3*. London: Centre for Excellence in Outcomes for Children (C4EO).

Campbell, B. (1988) *Unofficial Secrets: Child Sexual Abuse – The Cleveland Case*. London: Virago.

Cawson, P., Wattam, C., Brooker, S. and Kelly, G. (2000) *Child Maltreatment in the United Kingdom: A Study of the Prevalence of Child Abuse and Neglect*. London: NSPCC.

CEMACH (Confidential Enquiry into Maternal and Child Health) (2008) *Why Children Die*. London: CEMACH.

Cleaver, H., Nicholson, D., Tarr, S. and Cleaver, D. (2008) *Child Protection, Domestic Violence and Parental Substance Misuse: Family Experiences and Effective Practice*. London: DCSF.

Corby, B. (2006) *Child Abuse: Towards a Knowledge Base*, 3rd edn. Maidenhead: Open University Press.

CQC (Care Quality Commission) (2009) *Safeguarding Children: A Review of the Arrangements in the NHS for Safeguarding Children*. London: CQC.

CWDC (Children's Workforce Development Council) (2009) *Early Identification of Needs, Assessment and Intervention: The Common Assessment Framework for Children and Young People, A Guide for Practitioners*. Leeds: CWDC.

Daniel, B., Taylor, J. and Scott, J. (2009) *Noticing and Helping the Neglected Child*. London: DCSF.

DCSF (Department for Children, Schools and Families) (2009) *Referrals, Assessments and Children and Young People Who Are the Subject of a Child Protection Plan, England* – Year Ending 31 March 2009. London: DCSF.

DCSF/DH (Department for Children, Schools and Families/Department of Health) (2009) *Getting Maternity Services Right for Pregnant Teenage Teenagers and Young Fathers*. London: DCSF.

De Laar, F. and Lagro-Jansson, T. (2009) Child protection: a Dutch GP's perspective, in J. Taylor and M. Themessl-Huber (eds) *Safeguarding Children in Primary Health Care*. London: Jessica Kingsley.

Delargy, A., Shenker, D., Manning, J. and Rickard, A-J. (2010) *Swept Under the Carpet: Children Affected by Parental Alcohol Misuse*. London: Alcohol Concern.

DfE (Department for Education) (2010a) *Publication of Serious Case Review Overview Reports and Munro Review of Child Protection: Letter Dated 10th June 2010*. London: DfE.

DfE (Department for Education) (2010b) *Serious Case Review 'Child A'*. London: DfE.

DfES (Department for Education and Skills) (2004) *Every Child Matters: Change for Children*. London: DfES.

DH (Department of Health) (2000) *Framework for the Assessment of Children in Need and their Families*. London: The Stationery Office.

DH (Department of Health) (2003) *The Child's Plan*. London: DH.

DH (Department of Health) (2009) *You're Welcome: Quality Criteria Self-assessment Toolkit*. London: DH.

DH/DCSF (Department of Health, Department for Children, Schools and Families) (2009a) *Healthy Child Programme: Pregnancy and the First Five Years*. London: DH.

DH/DCSF (Department of Health, Department for Children, Schools and Families) (2009b) *Healthy Child Programme from 5–19 Years Old*. London: DH.

DH/DfES (Department of Health/Department for Education and Skills) (2006) *Looking for a School Nurse?* London: DH.

DHSSPS (Department of Health, Social Services and Public Safety) (2003) *Co-operating to Safeguard Children*. Belfast: Northern Ireland: DHSSPS.

Dingwall, R., Eekalaar, J. and Murray, T. (1983) *The Protection of Children: State, Intervention and Family Life*. Oxford: Blackwell.

Easton, C., Morris, M. and Gee, G. (2010) *LARC2: Integrated Children's Services and the CAF Process*. Slough: NFER.

Eckenrode, J., Campa, M., Luckey, D. *et al.* (2010) Long-term effects of prenatal and infancy nurse home visitation on the life course of youths, *Archives Pediatric Adolescent Medicine*, 164(1): 9–15.

Felitti, V.J., Anda, R.F., Nordenberg, D. *et al.* (1998) Relationship of childhood abuse and household dysfunction to many of the leading cause of death in adults: the Adverse Childhood Experiences (ACE) study, *American Journal of Preventative Medicine*, 14(4): 245–58.

Ferguson, L. (2009) Proactive in protection: a public health approach to child protection, in J. Taylor and M. Themessl-Huber (eds) *Safeguarding Children in Primary Health Care.* London: Jessica Kingsley.

Fleming, P., Blair, P., Sidebotham, P. and Haylor, T. (2004) Investigating sudden unexpected deaths in infancy and childhood and caring for bereaved families: an integrated multi-agency approach, *British Medical Journal,* 328: 331–4.

Fox, J. (2008) *A Contribution to the Evaluation of Recent Developments in the Investigation of Sudden Unexpected Deaths in Infancy.* Guildford: University of Surrey/National Policing Improvement Agency.

FSID (Foundation for the Study of Infant Deaths) (2010) *Child Death Review: A Guide for Parents and Carers.* London: DCSF.

Gardner, R. (2008) *Developing an Effective Response to Emotional Harm and Neglect in Children.* Norwich: University of East Anglia and NSPCC.

Gaw, S. (2000) *What Works With Parents With Learning Disabilities?* Basildon: Barnardo's Publications.

Geib, A-J., Babu, K., Ewald, M. and Boyer, E. (2006) Adverse effects in children after unintentional buprenorphine exposure, *Pediatrics,* 118: 1746–51.

Gilbert, R., Kemp, A., Thoburn, J. *et al.* (2008) Recognising and responding to child maltreatment, *The Lancet,* DOI:10.1016/S0140-6736(08)61707-9, accessed 23 January 2010.

Godeau, E., Nic Gabhainn, S., Vignes, C. *et al.* (2008) Contraceptive use by 15 year-old students at their last sexual intercourse: results from 24 countries, *Archives of Pediatric Adolescent Medicine,* 162(1): 66–73.

Golden, M., Samuels, M.P. and Southall, D.P. (2003) How to distinguish between neglect and deprivational abuse, *Archives of Disease in Childhood,* 88: 105–7.

Haringey Safeguarding Children Board (2009) *Serious Case Review: Baby Peter,* www.haringeylscb.org/executive_summary_peter_final.pdf, accessed 3 July 2010.

HM Government (2004) *Every Child Matters: Change for Children.* London: DfES.

HM Government (2008a) *Staying Safe: Action Plan.* London: DCSF.

HM Government (2008b) *Information Sharing: Guidance for Practitioners and Managers.* London: DCSF.

HM Government (2008c) *Safeguarding Children in Whom Illness is Fabricated or Induced. Supplementary Guidance to Working Together to Safeguard Children.* London: DCSF.

HM Government (2008d) *Safeguarding Children Who May Have Been Trafficked.* London: DCSF.

HM Government (2009) *Safeguarding Children and Young People from Sexual Exploitation* London: DCSF.

HM Government (2010) *Working Together to Safeguard Children: A Guide to Inter-Agency Working to Safeguard and Promote the Welfare of Children.* London: DCSF.

Humphreys, C. and Stanley, N. (2006) *Domestic Violence and Child Protection: Directions for Good Practice.* London: Jessica Kingsley.

Jenny, C. and Isaac, R. (2006) The relationship between child death and child maltreatment, *Archives of Disease in Childhood,* 91: 265–9.

Laming, Lord (2003) *The Victoria Climbié Inquiry: Report of an Inquiry by Lord Laming,* Cm 5730. London: The Stationery Office.

Laming, Lord (2009) *The Protection of Children in England: A Progress Report.* London: The Stationery Office.

Loughrey, C., Preece, M. and Green, A. (2005) Sudden unexpected death in infancy (SUDI), *Journal of Clinical Pathology,* 58: 20–1.

Morrison, T. (2009) The role of the scholar-facilitator in generating practice knowledge to inform and enhance the quality of relationship-based social work practice with children and families, doctoral thesis, University of Huddersfield.

Murray, M. and Osborne, C. (2009) *Safeguarding Disabled Children: Practice Guidance*. London: DCSF and The Children's Society.

Myers, J. Berliner, L., Briere, J. *et al.* (2002) *The APSAC Handbook on Child Maltreatment*, 2nd edn. London: Sage.

National Commission of Inquiry into the Prevention of Child Abuse (1996) *Childhood Matters*, Vols I and II. London: The Stationery Office.

NCCWCH (National Collaborating Centre for Women's and Children's Health) (2009) *When to Suspect Child Maltreatment*. London: RCOG Press.

Nelson, S. (2009) Preparing for the special challenge of sexual abuse, in J. Taylor and M. Themessl-Huber (eds) *Safeguarding Children in Primary Health Care*. London: Jessica Kingsley.

NHS Institute for Innovation and Improvement (2008) *Focus on: Children and Young People Emergency and Urgent Care Pathway*. Coventry: NHS Institute for Innovation and Improvement.

NICE (National Institute for Health and Clinical Excellence) (2007) *Methadone and Buprenorphine for the Management of Opioid Dependence: NICE Technology Appraisal Guidance 114*. London: NICE.

NMC (Nursing and Midwifery Council) (2006) *Standards for the Preparation and Practice of Supervisors of Midwives*. London: NMC.

NMC (Nursing and Midwifery Council) (2008) *The Code: Standards of Conduct, Performance and Ethics for Nurses and Midwives*. London: NMC.

NMC (Nursing and Midwifery Council) (2009a) *Guidance on Professional Conduct for Nursing and Midwifery Students*. London: NMC.

NMC (Nursing and Midwifery Council) (2009b) *Record-keeping: Guidance for Nurses and Midwives*. London: NMC.

NMC (Nursing and Midwifery Council) (2010) *Strategic Context Report*. London: NMC.

NPSA (National Patient Safety Agency) (2010) *National Framework for Reporting and Learning from Serious Incidents Requiring Investigation*. London: National Reporting and Learning Service/NPSA.

OECD (Organization for Economic Cooperation and Development) (2009) *Doing Better for Children*, www.oecd.org/els/social/childwellbeing, accessed 6 March 2011.

Office of the First Minister and Deputy First Minister Northern Ireland (2006) *Our Children and Young People – Our Pledge: A Ten Year Strategy for Children and Young People in Northern Ireland 2006–2016*. Belfast: OFMDFM.

Office of the First Minister and Deputy First Minister Northern Ireland (2009) *Safeguarding Children: A Cross-Departmental Statement on the Protection of Children And Young People*. Belfast: Children and Young People's Unit.

Office of the Children's Commissioner/Young Minds (2007) *Pushed into the Shadows: Young People's Experiences of Adult Mental Health Facilities*. London: Office of the Children's Commissioner.

Olds, D.L., Henderson, C.R. and Kitzman, J. (1994) Does prenatal and infancy nurse home visitation have enduring effects on qualities of parental caregiving and child health at 25 to 50 months of life? *Pediatrics*, 93: 1, 89–98.

Olds, D.L., Eckenrode, J., Henderson, C.R. *et al.* (1997) Long-term effects of home visitation on maternal life course and child abuse and neglect, *Journal of the American Medical Association*, 278(8): 637–43.

Polnay, J., Polnay, L., Lynch, M. and Shabde, N. (eds) (2007) *A Child Protection Reader*. London: RCPCH.

Powell, C. (2007) *Safeguarding Children and Young People: A Guide for Nurses and Midwives*. Maidenhead: Open University Press.

Pritchard, C. and Williams, R. (2009) Comparing Possible 'Child-Abuse-Related-Deaths' in England And Wales with the Major Developed Countries 1974–2006: Signs Of Progress? *British Journal Social Work (Advanced Access)*, 1–19, doi:10.1093/bjsw/bcp089.

Queen's Nursing Institute (2007) *Facing the Future: A Review of the Roles of Health Visitors*. London: DH.

RCP/RCPCH (Royal College of Pathologists, Royal College of Paediatrics and Child Health) (2004) *Sudden Unexpected Death in Infancy: A Multi-Agency Protocol for Care and Investigation. The Report of a Working Group Convened by the Royal College of Pathologists, Royal College of Paediatrics and Child Health* (The Kennedy Report). London: Royal College of Pathologists, Royal College of Paediatrics and Child Health.

RCPCH (Royal College of Paediatrics and Child Health) (2006) *Child Protection Companion*. London: RCPCH.

RCPCH (Royal College of Paediatrics and Child Health) (2008) *The Physical Signs of Child Sexual Abuse: An Evidence-based Review and Guidance for Best Practice*. London: RCPCH.

RCPCH (Royal College of Paediatrics and Child Health) (2009) *Fabricated or Induced Illness by Carers (FII): A Practical Guide for Paediatricians*. London: RCPCH.

RCPCH/RCN (Royal College of Paediatrics and Child Health, Royal College of Nursing) (2010) *Maximising Nursing Skills in Caring for Children in Emergency Departments*. London: RCPCH.

Reder, P., Duncan, S. and Gray, M. (1993) *Beyond Blame: Child Abuse Tragedies Revisited*. London: Routledge.

Robert, K. and Harris, J. (2002) *Disabled People in Refugee and Asylum Seeking Communities*. Bristol: The Policy Press.

Royal College of Psychiatrists (2004) *Behavioural Problems and Conduct Disorder: Factsheet*. London: RCP.

Royal College of Radiologists/RCPCH (2008) *Standards for Radiological Investigations in Cases of Suspected Non-accidental Injury*. London: RCPCH.

SCIE (Social Care Institute for Excellence) (2005) *Research Briefing 9: Preventing Teenage Pregnancy in Looked After Children*, www.scie.org.uk/publications/briefings/briefing09/index.asp, accessed 3 July 2010.

Scottish Executive (2004) *Protecting Children and Young People: Framework for Standards*. Edinburgh: Scottish Executive.

Sheridan, M., Sharma, A. and Cockerill, H. (2008) *From Birth to Five Years: Children's Developmental Progress*. London: Routledge.

Sidebotham, P. and Heron, J. (2006) Child maltreatment in the 'children of the nineties': a cohort study of risk factors, *Child Abuse and Neglect*, 30(5): 497–522.

Sidebotham, P., Fox, J., Horwath, J., Powell, C. and Perwez, S. (2008) *Preventing Childhood Deaths: A Study of 'Early Starter' Child Death Overview Panels in England*. London: DCSF.

Sidebotham, P., Brandon, M, Powell, C. *et al.* (2010) *Learning from Serious Case Reviews: Report of a Research Study on the Methods of Learning Lessons Nationally from Serious Case Reviews*. London: DfE.

Stein, M., Rees, G., Hicks, L. and Gorin, S. (2009) *Neglected Adolescents: A Review of the Research and the Preparation of Guidance for Multi-Disciplinary Teams and a Guide for Young People*. London: DCSF.

Strathearn, L., Mamun, A., Najman, J. and O'Callaghan, M. (2009) Does breastfeeding protect against substantiated child abuse and neglect? A 15-year cohort study, *Pediatrics*, 123: 483–93.

Taylor, J., Spencer, N. and Baldwin, N. (2000) Social, economic and political contexts of parenting, *Archives of Disease in Childhood*, 82: 113–20.

The Princess Royal Trust for Carers/The Children's Society (2010) *Supporting Young Carers: A Resource for Schools*. London: The Princess Royal Trust for Carers.

TPIAG (Teenage Pregnancy Independent Advisory Group) (2009) *Annual Report 2008–2009*. London: DCSF.

Underdown, A. (2000) *When Feeding Fails*. London: The Children's Society.

Vincent, S. (2009) *Child Death and Serious Case Review Processes in the UK*. Edinburgh: University of Edinburgh/ NSPCC.

WAG (Welsh Assembly Government) (2007) *Safeguarding Children: Working Together Under the Children Act 2004*. Cardiff: WAG.

WCPSRG/NSPCC (Welsh Child Protection Systematic Review Group, National Society for the Prevention of Cruelty to Children) (2008) *Core-Info: Thermal Injuries on Children*. Cardiff: University of Cardiff.

WCPSRG/NSPCC (Welsh Child Protection Systematic Review Group, National Society for the Prevention of Cruelty to Children) (2009a) *Core-Info: Bruises on Children*. Cardiff: University of Cardiff.

WCPSRG/NSPCC (Welsh Child Protection Systematic Review Group, National Society for the Prevention of Cruelty to Children) (2009b) *Core-Info: Head and Spinal Injuries in Children*. Cardiff: University of Cardiff.

WHO (World Health Organization) (2006) *Preventing Child Maltreatment: A Guide to Taking Action and Generating Evidence*. Geneva: WHO and International Society for Prevention of Child Abuse and Neglect.

WHO Health Evidence Network (2010) What are the most effective strategies for reducing rates of teenage pregnancies? www.euro.who.int/en/what-we-do/data-and-evidence/health-evidence-network-hen/publications/evidence-summaries-of-network-members-reports/what-are-the-most-effective-strategies-for-reducing-the-rate-of-teenage-pregnancies, accessed 3 July 2010.

Wright, C.M. (2005) What is weight faltering (failure to thrive) and when does it become a child protection issue? in J. Taylor and B. Daniel (eds) *Child Neglect: Practical Issues for Health and Social Care*. London: Jessica Kingsley.

Index

Locators shown in *italics* refer to figures and tables.

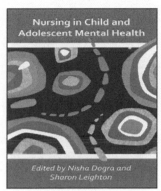

NURSING IN CHILD AND ADOLESCENT MENTAL HEALTH

Nisha Dogra and Sharon Leighton (Eds)

9780335234639 (Paperback)
2009

eBook also available

"Nurses have a key role to play within the Child and Adolescent Mental Health Team. Yet there are few textbooks devoted to the specialist and advanced roles which many undertake within this field of practice. This text will fill the void addressing legal and ethical issues while focusing upon clinical practice and the application of theoretical concepts."
Fiona Smith, Adviser in Children's and Young People's Nursing, Royal College of Nursing, UK

Key features:

- Looks at definitions and consequences of mental health, illness and stigma
- Considers the effect of child and family development on mental health
- Chapters include case scenarios, clinical applications and boxes highlighting the key context issues

www.openup.co.uk

WORKING WITH ADULTS AT RISK FROM HARM

Margaret Greenfields, Roger Dalrymple and Agnes Fanning (Eds)

9780335241224 (Paperback)
September 2011

eBook also available

This comprehensive book uniquely acknowledges the overlap between different states of adult vulnerability within a range of health, social care and community contexts. The book looks beyond social work practice and legislative focus to examine the categories of 'at risk' and 'vulnerable adults'. These include often forgotten groups such as homeless people, prisoners and migrant workers.

Key features:

- Presents case studies and practice examples from work and vulnerable groups that are often overlooked
- Designed as a 'browsable' volume which can be read non-sequentially
- Illustrates how different states of vulnerability are frequently contingent upon one another

www.openup.co.uk

 **OPEN UNIVERSITY PRESS**
McGraw · Hill Education

COMMUNICATION SKILLS FOR ADULT NURSES

Sarah Kraszewski and Abayomi McEwen (Eds)

9780335237487 (Paperback)
2010

eBook also available

With an emphasis on practical application, this lively and accessible guide will help nurses to hone and develop their communication skills. It is full of examples from both a patient and a nurse perspective. The book gives nurses the tools to continue to develop and apply effective communication skills.

Key features:

- Includes examples of both good and poor practice from real life experiences
- Uses common scenarios, activity points and suggestions for practice
- Shows how good communication underpins the essence of care

www.openup.co.uk

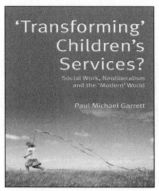

'TRANSFORMING' CHILDREN'S SERVICES
Social Work, Neoliberalism and the 'Modern' World

Paul Michael Garrett

9780335234257 (Paperback)
2009

eBook also available

"This is an excellent book and one of the best I have read for some time. It is a must have for all social work and social policy students and practitioners. Policy makers and managers should also read and digest this, even though they will probably find large parts an uncomfortable read."
Steve Rogowski, Professional Social Work (Dec, 2009)

Key features:

- Includes The Laming Report which examined the death of Victoria Climbié and its implications
- Addresses a range of issues of direct concern to practitioners
- Provides an accessible overview of the 'transformation' of Children's Services in England

www.openup.co.uk

OPEN UNIVERSITY PRESS
McGraw · Hill Education